IN PRAISE OF
OUR FATHERS
AND
OUR MOTHERS

IN PRAISE OF OUR FATHERS AND OUR MOTHERS

A Black Family Treasury by Outstanding Authors and Artists

Compiled by Wade Hudson and Cheryl Willis Hudson

JUST US BOOKS, INC.
East Orange, New Jersey

For my mother, Ma'dear, Lurline Jones Hudson,
and my father, Wade Hudson, Sr.
—WH

For my mother, Lillian Watson Willis,
and in memory of my father, Hayes Elijah Willis, III
—CWH

In Praise of Our Fathers and Our Mothers
A Black Family Treasury by Outstanding Authors and Artists
compiled by Wade Hudson and Cheryl Willis Hudson,
introduction and compilation copyright © 1997 by Wade Hudson and Cheryl Willis Hudson,
published by Just Us Books, Inc. copyright © 1997.

First Edition 10 9 8 7 6 5 4 3 2 1 Printed in Hong Kong

Library of Congress Number 96-76531
Cataloging-in-publication data is available.

ISBN 0-940975-59-9

JUST US BOOKS
East Orange, New Jersey

Contents

Introduction

Several years ago during an evening out with friends, the conversation turned to the family and the myriad problems it faces today. We talked about everything from unemployment to drug addiction and gang violence; from teen-age pregnancies to the incredible number of female-headed households. Along with our friends, we lamented what has been conveniently called the "breakdown" of far too many families and communities. We shuddered to think what the future held unless positive changes were vigorously pursued.

At home later that evening, the two of us continued the discussion. We recalled how different it was when we were growing up in the 1950s and 1960s in segregated Louisiana and Virginia. We both had strong parents, and our communities, to a large extent, were like extended families. There, we were nurtured, trained, encouraged, and prodded toward excellence and toward excellent goals.

But what was it like for other Black people? we wondered. In what kinds of environments were they reared? Just how important was family in their lives? What kind of stories did they have to tell?

The idea for *In Praise of Our Fathers and Our Mothers* was born that night.

Many of our friends and associates are writers and visual artists. Wouldn't it be interesting, we thought, to have some of them recount memories and create images about the impact their parents and families had on their lives?

This question evolved into a wish list, and we began approaching people about our book idea. They all seemed as excited and enthusiastic as we were. A book like *In Praise of . . .*, they agreed, was needed, not only for young people, but for people of all ages. Joyce

Hansen, Walter Dean Myers, Tom Feelings, Ashley Bryan, Floyd Cooper, Patricia and Fredrick McKissack, Leo and Diane Dillon, Haki Madhubuti, George Ford, Nikki Grimes, Virginia Hamilton, and the others also welcomed the opportunity to be part of a project that included the work of writers and artists whom they admired and respected.

We were moved by the scope and variety of the work submitted by some four dozen writers and visual artists. Each work is a unique and personal testament to the strength, durability, and importance of family, and parents in particular. After reviewing all the contributions we knew we had selected the perfect title for our book: *In Praise of Our Fathers and Our Mothers: A Black Family Treasury by Outstanding Authors and Artists.*

In spite of laments about the state of the family, we are assured that millions of Black fathers and mothers are still influencing their children in positive ways. They are working hard to provide environments important for the development of healthy children and strong, responsible adults.

A Liberian proverb states, "If you have a praise singer, your fame will spread." Our aim is to spread the good news and to affirm, through this collection, what we know to be true.

—Wade Hudson and Cheryl Willis Hudson

A Good Thing

by Candy Dawson Boyd

Thank you, Father
Thank you, Mother
For making Black
a good thing.
For teaching me
To think straight
And do battle against evil.
Keep the promise
To our 100 million kin
Long gone, yet near.
Walk the world
Writing my words.
Wear my skin
Like the continent it is.
Thank you,
For reaching deep inside
Through the frostline,
Holding me in one hand
And your love in the other,
Making Black
a good thing.

Bert James Smiled

by Elizabeth Fitzgerald Howard
illustration by Anna Rich

Sure, children, I'll tell you a story. You want to hear about your great grandma Bertha. My mother. She told me some things. And I heard some things. And I lived some things . . . about your great grandma Bertha. Called Bert.

Bert, they called her.

Short for Bertha.

Her baptism name was Bertha McKinley James (born the very day President McKinley was inaugurated: March 4, 1897).

But they called her Bert.

Bert James.

Mama Sarah's youngest child.

Big sister Flossie and big brother Brad took care of little Bert. Papa died when Bert was only eight. Mama Sarah sewed dresses for rich White ladies. Mama Sarah's fingers got sore and her eyes got so tired. "I'm going to be a teacher, Mama," Flossie said. "Me, too, Mama," said little Bert.

Little Bert James.

Now the family sure didn't have much money.

Mama Sarah had some help from her brother, Uncle Jimmy. He owned that fine grocery store.

"Uncle Jimmy has the best crabs in his store," Bert said.

Bert was proud of Uncle Jimmy's store.

Proud of Mama.

Proud of being Bert.

She grew up pert and perky as her name.

Bert James.

Always smiling.

And so pretty, too.

Ooh, was she pretty!

Studied hard.

Good marks in school.

High marks on all the teacher tests.

Opened a letter one morning and ran to find Mama. "Mama, I have a job! I'm to teach third grade!"

Mama was proud of Bert.

Bert had fun, too. Played basketball . . . Only five foot two, she was. That's all. But she was a star on that team. Even went to Washington to play basketball. And only five foot two.

But she was so quick.

So wiry.

So smiley.

So lively.

And pert.

Pert Bert.

Bert James.

Now you know there were lots of boys coming to call.

There was Calvin.

And Hugh.

And Pinky.

And Joe.

And there was Mac Fitzgerald.

Bert sure caught Mac's eye.

And he shone in hers, too.

Oh, yes. Mac.

He went to Harvard College, up north.

His pa was a lawyer.

Mac was gentle and soft.

Told little jokes.

Didn't talk much.

But talked enough–said, "Will you marry me, Bert?"

Too bad for Calvin and Hugh and Pinky and Joe.

Guess probably they wiped secret tears on their sleeves.

Bert James getting married . . .

Quiet wedding . . . Mama Sarah had died just the year before . . . Quiet wedding.

Bert's dress color called "ashes of roses." And ooh, the wedding gifts. Fancy French style furniture for the bedroom . . . silver . . . china . . . everything nice.

Honeymoon in Atlantic City. Of course.

Everybody went to Atlantic City for their honeymoon. No big fancy hotel if you were colored, though. Bert and Mac stayed at Cousin Julia's house. Walked on the boardwalk. Smiled. Soaked up sunny February days. Seemed like the sun would shine forever.

Went on back home to their school teaching jobs.

But maybe, maybe a small cloud was coming.

"I just don't like trying to make those big boys listen," Mac said. "They just don't care." Mac was not happy. Teaching high school was not for him. Joined his dad in his real estate office.

Guess the clouds went away.

And then a happy happy thing!

Someone new!

Guess who!

Baby Beppy. Yes, I was that baby.

Born at Christmas time.

"That's some baby," people said. They smiled at Beppy in her English style carriage with the pink silk pillow and blanket.

"Look at those rosy cheeks," said Miz Alice Hall. "Bert, did you put rouge on that baby's cheeks?"

Bert laughed. "No, Miz Alice, those are just her own rosy cheeks."

That's some baby, they said. "Born with a silver spoon in her mouth!" You know what that means? Everything perfect.

Bert and Mac and Beppy and everything perfect.

But not perfect.

Sun was not so bright now. Clouds coming in. Times were changing. Working in real estate with Pa isn't anything, Mac thought. I can do more, he thought. "Let's go to Boston," Mac said. "I can get a job there. And there will be good schools for Beppy."

"We can go, Mac," said Bert. Of course, she smiled.

Bert and Mac packed everything. Packed Beppy. And went north. Back north. Mac liked it there. Could breathe. Could do things his way. Thought he could. But tough times came. Tough times everywhere. You heard of the Great Depression?

Money was scarce.

Mac's new job didn't last.

"You're pretty light colored. If you could pretend you're not Negro I can recommend you to one of the banks," the adviser at Mac's college told him.

"No," said Mac.

Money scarcer.

Rent too high.

And a new baby now.

Babs. (You know your Aunt Babs!)

Tough times for Mac and Bert.

For pert Bert.

But Bert just smiled.

"It's O.K., Poogie," she said to Mac. That was the special sweet name. She called him Poogie. He called her Poogie, too. "It's

O.K. I have you and you have me and we have Beppy and Babs. I can find work. We'll be O.K."

But where?

No teaching job for Bert.

But she could try something else.

She could paint.

Got a job painting greeting cards.

And Mac found jobs sometimes. Different jobs.

It was O.K.

But the rent.

"Poogie," Bert said to Mac one day. "Poogie, I have heard of a place to live where we shouldn't have to pay so much rent. Just two rooms."

Mac wasn't sure. Just two rooms?

"We'll just store our furniture and silver and china," said Bert. "We'll be O.K." Sure, she smiled anyway.

"It's only for a while," Mac said. "I'll get a good job soon."

But Mrs. Ella Ford's house was nice.

"Your two rooms are in the attic," she said. "And mind you, I'm probably crazy to rent to a family with children."

"Babs and Beppy will be quiet," Bert said.

That's how we moved to the Castle. I called it the Castle. Up on top of a hill in the middle of the street. Other roomers on the second floor.

"It's like a castle," Beppy said. I said that. It was big like a castle. From the attic windows you could see the whole kingdom. And Babs and Beppy were princesses. Mrs. Ford was the witch saying *SSSSHHHH*.

"You are the king, Daddy," Babs told Mac. "And you are the queen, Mommy," Beppy told Bert.

Quick Bert cooking dinner after she came home from painting cards; lively Bert running down to wash clothes in the dark damp cellar after dinner; smiling Bert reading stories to Beppy and Babs and tucking us in after our prayers . . . *SHHH, Shhh* . . . Shushing Bert, keeping her promise that we would not disturb the other roomers.

"One day we'll have our own house," Bert said. "And we can bring back our French style bedroom furniture. And our silver. And our china. And you girls won't have to be so quiet."

"It's just for a while," Mac said.

Bert smiled. "We'll be fine," she said.

Years passed.

Beppy was in the first grade, second grade, third grade, fourth grade, fifth grade, sixth grade, seventh grade, eighth grade. There were blizzards and steamy hot days. There was a fierce hurricane. And a terrible polio epidemic. And summer train trips to Lulu's house. And Christmas came and went and came and came. But Mrs. Ford's castle was still home. And Bert was still smiling.

"What *is* French style furniture, Mommy?" Babs asked.

"You'll see it one day. Before we're all old and gray." Bert laughed at her rhyme.

Then, a letter arrived from Lulu. "Dear Bert and Mac, I am selling my house in the country. I am moving to Boston. I will live with you at Mrs. Ella Ford's. And we will look for a house to buy for us all."

Bert was so happy. So happy.

She grabbed Mac's hands and they danced around the room. "Oh, Poogie!" she said.

"We are going to have our own house. And, girls," she called to Babs and Beppy, "it won't be long now. You'll see that French style bedroom suite soon!"

A year later Bert and Mac and Beppy and Babs and Lulu had found their own house. Beppy and Babs felt sort of sad saying good-bye to the Castle. "We were princesses," said Babs. "But now we're real," said Beppy. "We'll each have our own bedroom!" And at last Mac and Bert could sleep in their French style bed. But the silver was saved for Sunday dinner and the fancy china for Thanksgiving and Christmas. Sometimes Mac had a job and other times he didn't. He wrote some short stories. And a couple of hundred pages of a novel.

Bert kept working but she wasn't painting cards. She was a clerk for the Commonwealth.

Beppy and Babs grew up and went to college and got married and moved away.

Healthy, smart, generous, caring Lulu lived to be 96 years old.

One day I asked Bert, "Mom, of everything that's happened to you, what was the best? What made you the happiest?" And she said, "Well, the second best thing that happened was moving into our house. But the best thing of all was marrying Mac."

"Oh, Mom," I said, "what about us? Babs and me?"

Bert smiled.

"Well, where did you come from, sugar pie?" she asked. ■

Legacy

by Ashley Bryan

As I neared completion of the paintings for a children's book of poems, I started sketches for *In Praise of Our Fathers and Our Mothers.* It has been on my mind throughout this year of travels. I had made little notes, but sitting in my home, looking around me, I put all those ideas aside.

I decided to draw directly from the collection that surrounds me . . .

On the bottom shelf of each linoblock print is a photograph of my parents. One is of my mother with a grandchild. The other is of my mother and father.

My parents inspired in their six children and the three cousins they raised when my aunt died, a love of creating beautiful things and of expressing that love in responding to beautiful things that others create as well.

We grew up during the Great Depression and lived in railroad apartments. My mother made our home so beautiful that our friends loved to visit. I remember that legacy to this day and try to express it in my work and in my home.

Legacy

by Ashley Bryan

Gifts From My Parents

by Margery Wheeler Brown

When John L. Wheeler and Margaret Hervey Wheeler moved with their children to Northeast Atlanta in 1912, they joined a tightly knit group of Black families who were already beginning to shape the character of the southern Black middle class. The Wheelers moved to Johnson Avenue, where many of their neighbors were doctors, ministers, educators, and businessmen: among them, the Trents, the Faulkners, the Dobbses, the Burneys. Atlanta, with its five Black colleges and growing Black-owned businesses, was a mecca for many.

In those days when there were no hotel accommodations for people of color, many Black Atlantans opened their homes as guest stops to visiting leaders. The Wheeler home was one of these, and those interesting visitors left an indelible mark on the Wheeler children, who as adults made their own contributions to their communities. Ruth, the eldest, was a pianist and music teacher and frequent accompanist to Black classical artists who gave concerts in Atlanta. John Hervey became a banker and lawyer who was in the forefront of the struggle for racial equality. The youngest child, Margery, became an artist, a teacher, and an author of children's books.

n the auditorium of Bethel African Methodist Episcopal Church, friends and relatives have gathered to say goodbye to one of the most unforgettable characters I have known. He was my father. He dearly loved this church on busy Auburn Avenue where, for more than 42 years, he had spent the greater part of every working day, in the city of Atlanta, of which he was so proud.

After the service, friends come to speak to us, to press my mother's hand, to reminisce. There is no sadness in their voices, only retrospective appreciation for a life lived fully, with joy and simple satisfaction.

He had come to Atlanta in 1912 to manage the office of the North Carolina Mutual Life Insurance Company, a young Black business with headquarters in Durham, North Carolina. When he retired at the age of 81, he was a vice president and associate agency director of this now well-established and greatly expanded company.

There was little about my father's early life to predict any degree of success, nor the security of spirit he developed. John Wheeler was born a few years after the abolition of slavery near the little town of Nicholasville, Kentucky. His mother was an ex-slave in her early teens. He was orphaned before his third birthday and reared by relatives. As soon as he was old enough to hold small jobs, the burden of his support fell upon his shoulders. During Reconstruction, like so many young Negroes, fired by the flame of freedom, he was filled with a burning desire for education. After completing the limited schooling available in his community, he found a source of higher education in nearby Ohio, where a church-supported college for Negroes had been established.

Father worked as a hotel waiter and part-time teacher to meet expenses at Wilberforce College. It took longer that way. He was almost 30 years old when he received his degree. The next months were spent in graduate study at the University of Chicago before he accepted a teaching position at Kittrell College, a small church-supported school in North Carolina.

During summer vacations while at Wilberforce, my father often returned to Kentucky to teach in the public schools. This was farm country, and schools were open during the summer months so that children could help parents during spring planting and fall harvesting. One earnest student who caught his attention was a serious, dark-eyed girl. As he watched her grow to young womanhood, John Wheeler found himself becoming more and more attracted to her. In glowing terms he described the opportunities for extended education at Wilberforce. Margaret Hervey sadly confided that there was little chance she could continue her education: she had no funds and no one to give her financial assistance.

Undaunted, my father returned to Wilberforce, where he had formed strong ties with one of the faculty families. He persuaded this family to take my mother into their home where she could assist with

household duties and serve as tutor and companion to their young daughter. He also arranged for tuition aid from Wilberforce.

Upon finishing her term at Wilberforce, Margaret married John, and they returned to live on the campus of Kittrell College. He continued teaching, and she taught young children of the community.

These were happy years for my parents. But there were drawbacks. The small college depended on the contributions of churches for support, and a teacher's pay was sporadic and uncertain. Nevertheless, they remained there for 10 years, during which time my father was named president of the school. Two children were born while they were there, and my parents realized that their growing family needed more security than their present situation offered.

In 1908 John Wheeler left Kittrell College to join the North Carolina Mutual Life Insurance Company. The company was then 11 years old, and my father started at the bottom. But he learned quickly and rose rapidly. As he grew in his job, he once again had an opportunity to work with young people, guiding many into becoming competent, confident agents.

My mother was a strong-spirited woman, fiercely protective of her family and her values even when those values sometimes conflicted with changing mores. By nature she was quiet and reserved, a trait sometimes mistaken for aloofness. Those close to her knew her to be warm, generous, and deeply concerned about others. I remember the annual ritual of filling Christmas stockings for children in an orphanage, and the many days when I came home from school to find her packing a tray with a hot dinner for an ailing neighbor. The neighbor might be a close friend or just a "speaking acquaintance."

My mother and my father were good partners in parenting. Their early years as teachers set the tone of my childhood experiences. Mother taught us to read long before we were of school age, and read to us daily. She taught us to respect and admire language, written and spoken, and to glean from the strengths and weaknesses of those fictional characters important lessons for our own lives. King Arthur and the Knights of the Roundtable, Robin Hood and his Merry Men of Sherwood Forest, Oliver Twist, David Copperfield, and Tiny Tim were my childhood companions. We laughed with them, cried with them, and adopted their expressions as our own.

My father read to us also. I was never sure whether he read aloud for our benefit or simply to savor the content and music of the words. His subjects were different from those chosen by my mother. Father read to us from Shakespeare, Tennyson, and Longfellow, from Paul Laurence Dunbar, James Weldon Johnson, and other Black writers.

And he read to us from the Bible. He was a deeply religious man, yet I never heard him argue a religious point, nor did he try to impose his views on another, not even his own children. His reverence was quiet, and very much a part of his daily life. I can close my eyes and go back in time to hear him at the Sunday breakfast table reading his favorite Bible verse: "Now faith is the substance of things hoped for, the evidence of things not seen." It was the creed by which he lived.

I was quite young when I became aware of my father's capacity for enjoyment. The smallest act of being was a delight to him. On our block, early morning sweeping of porches and sidewalks was a daily ritual. With my little broom, I would join him. When we had finished, we would walk the length of the block, greeting each neighbor. On these walks he would teach me to see the things in nature which fascinated him, and by carefully removing any obstacle on the sidewalk lest "someone stumble over it," he taught me about thoughtfulness as well.

My father's enthusiasm for sports moved from college football to basketball to baseball. He attended local games and kept close tab on player and team records. He could count among his friends many young people who were involved in sports, and he was a familiar figure at regional tournaments. One of his prized possessions was a plaque presented to him for "Continuous Interest In Sports." Yet, in the few sports in which he participated, he was totally unaccomplished. He played tennis but was never good at the game; he looked forward to one or two days of hunting during the small game season, but was a poor marksman and bagged little.

We acquired our first car when my brother reached driving age. Father was never able to master the art of driving, but he sat with us through driving lessons and early morning practice sessions until each child was at ease behind the wheel. His lack of these several skills left him completely unperturbed and never seemed to dampen his enthusiasm for any of these activities.

When Father retired at 81, we were afraid that he would find the hours lagging heavily, but we needn't have been. He simply moved his activity from his offices in the Odd Fellows Building on Auburn Avenue to Auburn Avenue itself. Unless the weather absolutely forbade it, he made a daily circuit, stopping first at his former office to chat with co-workers. From there he would go to the YMCA, which he had seen grow from early frugal days to become the hub of the Black business community, pausing to speak encouragingly to the son of a friend. Father's progress was slow, for he was frequently stopped by passersby for a brief chat. The daily tour usually ended with lunch at a busy restaurant.

John Wheeler was extremely proud of Atlanta's growth and progress. With out-of-towners, he would launch into an enthusiastic description of the city's latest development, starting with "You've no idea how this town has grown!" We laughingly dubbed him "Atlanta's Ambassador At-Large." And his interest went deeper than words. Year after year he contributed to and worked in citywide civic campaigns, and for causes within the Black community. His greatest concern a few days before his death was his inability to attend the final meeting of the YMCA's financial drive.

My father died a few months before his 88th birthday. He left little in material assets. During his lifetime he had provided a modest but comfortable living for his family, and educated his three children, enabling each to earn a living in his or her chosen field. For him, that was the usefulness, the purpose of money. Although he had a clear understanding of finance, he had no interest in accumulating more than was needed for these purposes. But the legacy our parents left us had far greater value than material assets.

Early in our lives our mother introduced us to the world of books, freeing our imaginations to explore other places, other times. My father gave us the gift of wonder–not mere curiosity–but wonder, that this complex, interconnected, balanced universe, battered as it is by wars, by prejudices, by personal animosities, by fear and suspicion, still offers such an abundance of beauty and if we would only see it–love. ∎

Crack a Book!

words by Dayton Cooper

With a Name Like Steptoe . . .

Bweela and Javaka Talk
with Pat Cummings

*Bweela and Javaka Steptoe
may already be known to
readers of John Steptoe's
books as the stars of his wry
and affectionate* Daddy Is a
Monster . . . Sometimes.
*Because they are the children
of fine artist Stephanie
Douglas and illustrator/
author John Steptoe, whose
early brilliance led to a
career filled with awards
and honors, many wondered
if they would grow up to be
artists themselves. Pat
Cummings, herself a noted
children's book illustrator/
author who has known
Bweela and Javaka since
they were teenagers, explored
the extent to which their
lineage and upbringing had
influenced them when the
three got together for a talk
in the fall of 1995.*

Pat: First of all, what are you both doing now?

Javaka: I'm working at the Brooklyn Children's Museum doing a variety of programs. I create, write, and perform the programs. I explain the different galleries to the children, do arts and crafts with them, read stories, show them animals . . . whatever is needed.

Bweela: I'm still studying fashion design at FIT–Fashion Institute of Technology in New York City. I already have my associate's in fashion design and now I want my bachelor's. I specialize in knitwear and want to learn more about it . . . the construction of knits, how to sew knit garments . . . so I can design my own fabrics and make the actual garment.

Pat: Javaka, you recently graduated from Cooper Union. How was the "journey"?

Javaka: At Cooper I jumped all over the place. I studied print-making, video, and sculpture. Now, I'm focused on illustrating my first book. It's a collection of poetry about fathers . . . I guess right now I'm in transition. I'm getting out of the school frame of mind and coming into a frame of mind where I can do what I need to do as far as my work is concerned.

Pat: Entering reality?

Javaka: That's it.

Pat: To what extent do you think your parents influenced your career choices? Did it make any difference that your parents were both artists?

Javaka: Yeah! I used to draw superheroes and dinosaurs when I was little, and I just kept drawing. I once told my father I wanted to be a scientist and he said, "Why? You draw a lot, but I never saw you do a science project." I guess I might have taken a different road, but I would probably have ended up doing the same thing.

19

Bweela: I think my parents had a lot of influence on me. I always said, "I can't draw because I can't draw like my father draws." But after he died, I saw pictures that he had done when he was little and he couldn't draw either! After that, I thought, "Oh, I see you really do have to practice." I remember him making me draw, and it was like torture to me. I didn't want to draw.

Pat: He would sit you down and *make* you draw?

Bweela: Well, yeah. He would have us trace something and then keep trying to practice and draw it. He kept telling me, "If you want to be in fashion, you have to draw." And that was always an argument between us because I would say, "You don't have to draw to be a fashion designer. You can get a croqui, which is just a figure, and draw the clothing on top of the figure."

Javaka: My father used to make me do still lifes. We used to trace pictures off of records, to get the form, the shape of the figure, to learn how to blend colors . . . and things like that.

Pat: About how old were you when your father started having you do these exercises?

Bweela: Two years old! It was torture.

Javaka: Three months! The doctor slapped me, and my dad handed me a pencil. I always wanted to draw.

Pat: Did your mother have you try similar things?

Bweela: She would give us more things to do, besides just tracing. Both of our parents knew how to sew, so our father would make a lot of clothing. Our mother would let us do what we wanted to do–paint if we wanted to paint, or make something in clay. We even went to the Children's Art Carnival and got to do photography and pottery and sewing . . . a whole bunch of different things. I'm not saying our father was so strict, but our mother would more often let us do what we wanted.

Pat: Looking back, was your father trying to give you formal lessons?

Bweela: Well, I think he knew we were interested in art, or that I was interested in sewing. Since he knew that I was going to have to draw, I think he was just getting us used to the idea of drawing and learning. He wanted us to see what goes with what and how different things work. I think that's what he was trying to do.

Javaka: Also, it wasn't as though he would sit us down every Thursday and say, "Okay, kids, it's lesson time." It wasn't a scheduled thing at all but happened if he got in the mood to teach us.

Pat: Did your parents give you any advice that you still use?

Javaka: I wish that he had given me more information about the business aspect of making artwork. Even though he helped us with the drawing, if a contract came he would only say, "Just read the numbers." I don't know if that was because he didn't know much about business or because he just didn't think to relate that to us for another reason. Maybe he thought he would be around longer.

Bweela: I wish I had listened to my father about the drawing, because in school the teachers told me to do the same things that my father had. I could have already had it down pat if I had listened to him instead of fighting about it.

Pat: To what extent did you get involved in your father's work?

Bweela: A lot of times he would take us along when he went to see the publisher. I used to wonder how a book was made. As soon as he had an idea for a story, he would say, "Hey, I wrote this story. What do y'all think of this?" He always read it to us before he took it to the publisher. He would ask what we thought about it and then go from there. I would see him drawing the pictures and cutting out the words and pasting them into position and I'd ask, "How do they get them into book form?" When we went to the publishers, they would explain to us how the art got printed.

Pat: Were you exposed to the business of fine arts through your mother? Did you go to her shows?

Bweela: Yes, we'd go to my mother's shows. She was in a women's art group. She also illustrated a picture book once when we were really young, called *My Three Wishes*. I still have the book. She was always doing artwork. But maybe because she had another job and was also going to Pratt, her influence in terms of art wasn't as strong as our father's was.

Pat: When you were little, did you realize that what he did might be different from what other parents did?

Javaka: Yes! For one thing he was always home.

Pat: How did you feel about being models?

Javaka: Sometimes he would call us in from playing outside and say, "Here, hold this. Stand like this and don't move." Most of the time I wished I could stay outside playing. I remember him taking pictures for *Daddy Is a Monster . . . Sometimes*. I think my father went into the ice cream store before us and bribed some lady to buy us ice cream. We were feeling good because we had ice cream, and then he made Bweela drop hers. She had a fit! And he sat there and took pictures of it. I think Bweela still feels pain.

Bweela: No. I was upset that he wasted an extra ice cream! Once he told us to go in a room and play and mess up the beds. Now, this was fun. Who wouldn't want to tear up a room? But we gave him a hard time and said, "We don't want to have a pillow fight. We're tired."

Javaka: Yeah, because then we would have to clean it up.

Bweela: He would also take our giant Legos and say, "Pretend this is a horn." We were role-playing all the time. I guess most kids would be excited for their parents to be like that. My father used to joke, "We're not like the Cosby Show, we're not like those types of people."

Sometimes my father would just make an appointment with us to take pictures. It could be embarrassing. When he was doing *Mufaro's Beautiful Daughters*, he had me standing on 34th Street holding a razor in my hand and trying to act like it was a mirror. I said, "Daddy, everybody's staring at me." Later I had to pose in Central Park, and my friend who was with me said, "Oh my God, your father's making you dress up in sheets in the park!" I was in sixth grade and it was just annoying to me then.

Pat: But weren't you pleased when you saw yourself in the books?

Javaka: It was nice, but I would rather be playing because I was a kid.

Pat: Were you aware of his celebrity, of the attention he got because of his books?

Bweela: He was just a father and a pain at times. He was an artist, he did children's books . . . it was no big deal to me at the time.

Pat: Did you feel any pressure about doing your own artwork because he was a well-known artist?

Javaka: Yeah. Lots of times . . . Sometimes teachers would compare me to my father.

Pat: Did he ever do presentations at your schools?

Bweela: He came to my elementary school once. I guess that was the first time that I thought my father was really famous. Kids went "ooh" and "ahh"– even knocked down chairs to get to him. He was working on *Daddy Is a Monster . . . Sometimes* and he handed out copies of the book's pages to my class and signed autographs. Once, when I was in junior high school and Michael Jackson was really big, my dad drew a picture of him for me and wrote on

it, "Oh, Bweela!" I went to school and made photocopies and gave them to my friends saying, "Look what my father did, look what my father did!" That was a big thing to me because everyone loved Michael Jackson.

Pat: When he was actually working on his paintings did you watch them develop?

Bweela: He used to get mad at me because when he showed me something I'd only say, "That's nice," and go about my business. Now, it's funny. Everybody thinks I like *Mufaro's Beautiful Daughters* just because I'm in it, but I really like it for the artwork . . . because you can see every single line. I remember all the trouble that he went through on that book to make sure that he had the right pen, the right ink, the right this, or the right that. My favorite picture is the title page that has all the animals. I told him he should make it into a poster because he put so much effort into including the right African animals. Now when I look at it I think it's amazing. But growing up around his art, it was just the norm to us. When you're a little kid and from Day One your parents are into artwork, that's just how it is.

Pat: Do you go out with the books and talk to the kids now?

Bweela: At times. With me, because of *Mufaro's Beautiful Daughters*, kids think I'm really a princess. But they're shocked that I live in Brooklyn, that I live in a house. People think that we're fantasy, that we're not real. I guess that was a good thing about my father, that he used people that he knew, that he related to. I guess it was easier for him to draw what was close to him. Sometimes he would even combine two people that he knew, combine their features, making one person. Kids always ask, "How did he get the pictures into the book?" I try to explain to them how he used photographs to draw from, but that's a hard concept for children. Maybe they think he just waved his hands and pushed me into the books or something. They're just so amazed to see that you're real.

Pat: Did you two go through a rebellion phase when you were growing up? Did you ever feel a need to reject art as a career?

Javaka: I always felt like I wouldn't make big money doing art, that I'd probably have to make money by some other means.

Bweela: I never rebelled against choosing a creative career. I did rebel against the drawing part. But I didn't have any pressures about being like my father, since I was doing something completely different. He was happy with what he was doing. He always said that whatever you choose as your career should be something that you want to do, not something you have to drag yourself out of bed for.

Pat: Can you recognize in yourself certain strengths or weaknesses that came from your parents?

Javaka: My parents are very important to me. I'm basically a product of what they are, where they've come from. I have aspects of both of them. In figuring out who I am I need to know who my parents were and who their parents were. I like learning about my family history. I visited my grandfather's family in Jamaica and saw things about that side of the family that go on within me. They are third cousins but people mistook me for one of my cousin's sons!

In terms of strengths and weaknesses, I think I have my mother's durability. She's a very strong woman. She's kind of quiet and, between Bweela and myself, I'm probably most like my mother. I can be loud, but for the most part I'm quiet. Growing up, I held in a lot of things, which I try not to do anymore. I've become more open. I draw more like my father than my mother. Maybe that came from watching my father draw more. Evidently, he had a greater influence on my artwork.

Bweela: For me, some of the things my father did annoyed me, but now I find myself doing the same things. Even the way he would sit in a chair is the way I find myself sitting at times. I think I've picked up a lot from my mother . . . her versatility, for example. My father might do a couple of things like pottery, but my mother could do so much more than just draw. She holds everything inside but I'm a big mouth: "Here I am, everybody, look at me!" If I want something, I make sure everybody knows it. My father was like that, too.

When I was growing up, my mother would never talk to me about sex or ask me questions. My mother was more like my parent. My father seemed more like my friend. I couldn't tell him everything, but I could tell him more than I could my mother. So, I felt a bit more comfortable with my father. Even though we fought all the time, it was probably because we were so much alike. We both were stubborn, and both wanted to have our way. I think I did inherit a lot from my father. After he died, I got closer to my mother.

Pat: Losing a parent is traumatic. When your father died did you both feel resolved about your relationship with him?

Both: No.

Javaka: I wished I had spent more time with him and had learned more about his life. Basically, all I know about is the time I spent with him. There are so many people who could tell me things about when he did this or that, about when he was younger and wasn't a parent yet. The first couple of years after he died, I missed him a lot. Sometimes I would wish that I would see him walking down the street and that was a weird feeling. I never really understood the fact of somebody dying until my father died. Now, I can relate to how somebody's feeling. In that sense, you could say his death kind of opened me up.

I don't know that it made me closer to my mother, like Bweela. I'm a lot like my mother and, probably because of that, we're not as close. I love her and really care a lot about her, but I don't know much about what she does on a daily basis, what her work day is like.

Bweela: I really felt bad when he died, maybe even guilty about all the arguments we had. It was hard for me when he died.

As soon as we were told that he probably would die within the week, I just couldn't handle it. I had to leave. I felt like I should have done this, I should have done that. He didn't want to tell us when he was sick or that one day he was going to die. He didn't want us to treat him differently because he was dying. In a way you kind of wanted to treat him differently, but I'm glad I didn't.

Javaka: Oh, I think we did a bit. We distanced ourselves from him. I remember things like being in the house and whenever he would come upstairs, we would go downstairs. I remember he felt really bad about that.

Bweela: If you know you're sick, you may say you don't want anybody to treat you differently. But I think you do want people to treat you a little differently. Maybe he wanted that attention, and we weren't giving it to him because we felt bad about it. And now that he's gone, I don't have anybody to fight with, to tell me, "I bet you can't do that."

Pat: Do you think now that he might have said that in an attempt to challenge you, to provoke you to try harder?

Bweela: Maybe. He would tell Javaka, "I want you to know how to cook for yourself, because I don't want you to be some guy that marries a woman and expects her to do everything."

When I started dating he'd tell me not to let a guy pay too much . . . to sometimes pay for him, so that no one would have control over me. I think he did his job as a father . . . He may not have lived in luxury, but people knew him for what he had accomplished. I am even more proud of him now that I see how other people react to him and his work. I wish I had been able to tell my father that. We'd really like to keep his work alive and hope to preserve it by having exhibitions and by giving talks.

Pat: Did either of your parents give you any "words to live by"? Anything that stays with you?

Javaka: My mother's famous words were: "Look it up!" My father taught us how to make this stuff he called "Potato Good Stuff": potatoes, cheese, sausages, vegetables and . . . good stuff. All mixed together, like a casserole.

Bweela: We were lucky to have the parents that we had growing up. We were exposed to a lot. I remember saying, "If we see another museum, we'll burn it!" Because it was *always* museums, *always* art shows, *always* this, *always* that.

But now I realize that it was good to get exposed to things outside of the regular. We left the block a couple of times.

Pat: Do you have a vision of where you're headed with your work?

Bweela: I would only want to work for someone else for the experience, but not for the rest of my life. I want to have my own business designing clothing and accessories– shoes, hats, belts. With a name like Steptoe, I have to do shoes!

Javaka: Right now, I'd say that I'm in my transitional stage. In the next couple of years I just want to have a nice life. I went down to Virginia where we have family and I've been thinking I might go there and stay for a little while. I've been doing a lot of traveling and I've seen some stuff. New York is a very different place from the rest of the world. Eventually, I would like to be like Picasso and have a little house in Italy with big, big walls and sunshine coming in. I'd just sit in the courtyard and paint and talk and eat good food.

Pat: And sell paintings for billions of dollars to afford this lifestyle?

Javaka: Yeah, yeah. ∎

Flying

by *Richard Wesley*

illustration by *David J. A. Sims*

Sometime in 1953, when I was eight years old, my parents took my brother and me to the movies to see *The Bridges at Toko-Ri*, starring William Holden and Frederick March. The film, an adaptation of a popular novel by James Michener, was about the exploits of Navy fighter pilots during the Korean War. The wide-screen movie process known as Vista Vision had just been invented and Hi-Fidelity sound, a precursor to stereo, was all the rage. Now, when people went to the movies, images were sharper, brighter, more lifelike than ever before, and even the smallest sound could be magnified to the level of thunder of the gods.

Imagine then, the impact on an eight-year-old boy, staring up at the giant screen, seeing gleaming black jet fighters hurled by steam catapults into the air from the flight deck of the USS Lexington. Jet fighters going from 0 to 100 miles per hour across a wooden deck, a distance of less than 300 feet, then reaching speeds of nearly 500 miles an hour within minutes of takeoff. The **WHOOSH!** of the catapults, the **ROAR** of jet engines, the **CRASHING** of waves against the hull of the carrier as it plowed through the seas, the **EXCITED VOICES** of the flight deck commanders barking orders to the crew preparing plane after plane for takeoff–all of that controlled chaos, all of that **POWER!!**

My little eight-year-old self knew that flying a jet plane in the United States Navy from the deck of a mighty carrier had to be the highest calling to which any human being could aspire.

As I grew older, I learned everything I could about aircraft. I was soon able to identify many different types of planes by sight and could tell you everything about them, from their weight, wingspan, and speed, to their armament, if military aircraft, and load capacity, if civilian. I read books about the principles of flight and watched every TV documentary I could on the history of airplanes or the dynamics of aircraft design. When the Space Age began, I became aware that the first astronauts were also Navy and Air Force pilots. This only increased my determination to fly, for now, I knew, jet pilots could become astronauts and fly into space. Someday, I could fly to the stars!

Few kids in my neighborhood had such an ambition. It was a working-class neighborhood of factories, smelting plants, and oil refineries. Our fathers worked in those places, in tough union jobs, doing back-breaking labor that often left them exhausted at the end of their working day. It was expected that when our time came, we kids would take their places in those factories, and that our children would someday repeat our lives.

My parents saw things differently. Unlike many of our friends, my brother Len and I never got past the plant gate where my Dad worked, because he never allowed it. He didn't want us to know anything about the factory because he never wanted us to think about working there. Mom and Dad let us know from the day we entered kindergarten that they expected us to attend college and do great things. This was fine with me because the Navy expected all its pilots to be college graduates, and I was not going to disappoint the Navy.

But dreaming of being a pilot in my neighborhood was difficult. Most of my friends could not imagine that much. Poor people–especially poor Black people–did not fly planes, did not become astronauts, did not dream.

I was teased. I was sometimes dismissed as a hopeless egghead because I wanted to get good grades. Other kids called me "crazy" because of my dream to be a pilot instead of something "practical." Others thought I was stupid and wasting my time. But I never let anything dissuade me from my dream to fly. I held fast to my goal despite the laughter and snide remarks. And as I entered high school, my ambition to become a Navy fighter pilot grew stronger and stronger. With each passing birthday, it seemed nothing could stop me.

And then, two things happened: First, I took Algebra–and failed miserably. No matter how hard I tried to understand the concepts, I just couldn't master them. I ended up having to take the course over and squeaked through with a D. I didn't even bother with calculus and trigonometry.

During this time came the second blow to my dream of flying. I grew. And grew. And grew. Until finally I grew taller than Navy regulations allowed in the early 1960s. Cockpits in carrier-based fighter planes are smaller than those in Air Force jets. Therefore, the Navy tended to reject people who were taller than a certain height. Today, with larger jets, the height regulations are not quite as stringent and a person my height, over six feet, can fly with the Navy. But, in those days, it was not possible.

I was devastated. Even though I knew I could probably try for the Air Force after college, it was not the same to me. Air Force pilots did not sail on carriers, or take off from them. I had come to see landing and taking off from a carrier as the most challenging and exciting kind of flying there was. Though the Air Force probably had the superior aircraft, my gut told me they did not have the superior pilots. And I knew I didn't want to fly for the airlines–that would be boring.

At the age of 16, I had no idea what I wanted to do if I couldn't fly. No other occupation interested me. I wanted to travel; I wanted something that would allow me to meet new people and see new places. I wanted new challenges and adventure. And there was nothing I could see that offered all of that. I was a fairly good athlete in school, but I was not likely to ever play major league baseball or go to the NBA or NFL. Though I played the drums, I knew I was not good enough to join a band—and I certainly couldn't sing! No, nothing interested me like flying. I'd put everything I had into that one dream and now it would never come to pass.

One day, lamenting all of this to my mother, she asked me why I didn't think about writing, maybe even become a journalist. I shook my head and told her I doubted it. But she persisted, reminding me of some things my brother and I did as kids . . .

Len would put on one of my Dad's sports jackets and I would don Dad's trench coat and favorite dress hat. I'd get a blank piece of paper and write the word, *Press* on it, like they did in old movies, and then, suited up with a few other props of the trade, Len and I would head out to cover stories on our beat. We'd interview friends and neighbors, but most often my mother, and scribble notes down on our notepads. Then, on the kitchen table, we'd draw columns on blank pieces of notebook paper and, with pens, pencils, and markers, we went to press with the stories we'd collected. We even did headlines: **"FLASH! Mom Cooks Collard Greens for Dinner!"**

Other times, when we didn't have enough money to buy comic books, Len and I, and my best friend Michael, used to make up our own. Len and Mike usually did the artwork,

and I came up with the words. Our specialties were war stories (frequently about pilots, naturally), action heroes (Len was good at making them up), and science fiction (which all three of us loved).

I had forgotten all these things until Mom brought them up. But she was not finished there. She reminded me also that I was getting As and Bs in English and history and that I loved writing essays and book reports.

It was like a giant light went off inside my head. Of course she was right! After all, I loved watching live TV dramas like "Playhouse 90" and comedy programs like "Your Show of Shows" and "The Dick Van Dyke Show." I was absolutely crazy about the series "Twilight Zone," "The Defenders," and "The Outer Limits."

All the things I wanted—action, adventure, travel, meeting new people, overcoming obstacles and challenges, were there in the stories I could write. I could still soar—if not in the cockpit of a Navy jet fighter, then certainly on the wings of my imagination! By the time I graduated from high school, I knew that creative writing was what I wanted to do. My mother's words those many years ago put me on a road I have traveled ever since, through playwriting and screenwriting, and I have not looked back. ■

Bridges

by Walter Dean Myers
illustration by James E. Ransome

There are dreams to which we will always cling, which will always define the being we recognize as self. What we know of others are gathered memories, collages of events that live within us. In my life passages I remember the bridges that were my adoptive parents.

I was two and a half when the young woman who gave birth to me died, and not much older than that when I was sent to another family to be raised. I have no memory of the bus trip from West Virginia to Harlem, or of my first meeting with Herbert and Florence Dean, the only parents I have ever known. What I have known of these people, who I remember them to be, has changed over the years, coming most sharply into focus upon my father's death in 1986.

The last winter snow had finally melted and the tops of the trees were showing the first signs of new life when it became clear that he was failing. Each day my wife and I coaxed our old Maverick out to the East Orange Veteran's Hospital, the silence in the car was heavy with grief, for we knew that any visit might be the last. My wife had grown to care for my father, accepting his irascible ways and worrying about his diet much more than I ever did. Her visits to the hospital were selfless, filled with sympathy for both me and my father. My own concerns, viewed through the prism of distance, were not as pure. I, too, cursed the disease which had consumed his strength, which had destroyed this Black man from within as nothing had been able to do from without, but there was also something that I needed from him, one last gift before he went on his way. I needed his final approval, his blessing if you will, of the man I had become.

From my own maturity my father was an easy man to understand. Hard times were normal for Blacks in Baltimore, where he was born in 1907. By the age of 10 he was working full-time. His father was a tall, Bible-willed man who ran a horse and wagon hauling business, and when my father was a child his grandfather, in Virginia, still worked the land on which he had once been enslaved.

Like other poor children his age in those pre-World War I days, he found that good times and full bellies were few and far between. He developed a clear, useful wisdom. If you weren't willing to work for something, you really didn't want it. It was a philosophy, imprinted on him as he hauled wood through the streets of Baltimore, that both colored and shaped his life.

My Dad wasn't a man to take a lot of nonsense. He found himself in court as a teenager for knocking down a White southerner who ordered him off the sidewalk as the man's wife passed. He found himself in jail for shooting at a man who tried to cheat him out of a day's wages.

My adoptive mother had to be the best looking woman he ever met. Or is that my memory? Half Indian, half German, from a little community near Lancaster, Pennsylvania, Florence Gearhart had worked as a cook's helper from the time she was 13. What they had in common, I think, was the understanding of what it was to be poor in America, and the ambition to do better.

The decision to move to New York must have been an exciting one for them. My mother talked of her early days in Harlem as overwhelming. My father had done some work on the docks in Baltimore and quickly found the New York waterfront. It was easier for Blacks to get night work and he worked the docks when he could in the evenings and worked on one of the mobster Dutch Schultz's moving vans during the day. Mama did days work, cleaning homes. She used to tell me about the first years of their marriage with an excitement that escaped me. I didn't understand why my father would get mad because some piano player named Fats Waller paid Mama too much attention, or why she would get mad if he lost money gambling with a tap dancer by the name of Bojangles.

In my family there were no psychological inducements to behave properly. There were simply standards one learned by a tone of voice, a raised eyebrow, a significant pause. You respected all adults you met. You did not associate with anyone unworthy of respect. In the home you refrained from backtalk–and backtalk included sucking one's teeth, rolling one's eyes, and fixing one's mouth as if one wanted to say something fresh.

When my mother wasn't out working she was working around the house. She seemed to be always washing, dusting, or ironing something. I would follow her from room to room, as she never seemed to tire of talking to me. In the afternoon, the work done and the dinner started, she would read to me from *True Romances*. The heavy bosoms didn't mean much to me, but the sound of her voice in that spotless, sun-drenched Harlem kitchen did.

There was never a moment when a light bulb went off and I announced to the world that I could read. But somehow, by the time I was five, I was reading. I could handle *True Romances* all by myself.

By the time I reached Junior High School 43, I was officially listed as "bright." The reading that had begun with *True Romances* and comic books expanded. I read voraciously. I had begun to write. I had also begun to grow farther and farther away from my parents.

Why? What happened between us? I had changed, had grown through books and reading in ways unfamiliar to my parents.

High school brought new opportunities, and new problems. My tenth-grade reading included Thomas Mann, Honoré de Balzac, Eugene O'Neill, and Dylan Thomas. Reading was excellent to me, and so, increasingly, was writing. Dealing with ideas became an overt part of my consciousness. But there were other influences, viewed now from adult understanding, which affected me greatly. My father was working as a janitor/handyman. Everyone in the tenement in which I lived worked with their hands at menial jobs.

My parents began to represent to me what I did not want to be. I began to find my identity in the books and in the concept of myself as an "intellectual." Being "smart" became the refuge from the notion of the Black inferiority that was being offered to me in school and in the general society and which I had, unconsciously, accepted. I was crushed when I discovered that I would not be able to go to college.

It had been a sacrifice for my parents to maintain me in high school, and they simply could not afford to keep a growing young man in school, without help. In a fit of teenaged angst, I dropped out of school. I welcomed the trouble to be found in the streets of Harlem, deliberately defying the family tenets, rejecting the values I felt had rejected me. In effect, I dropped out of my father's world.

My father and I became cautious friends when I reached my mid-20s, and closer friends after my mother died. But still there was a gap between us, a distance between us that I couldn't understand. I had overcome my juvenile hostility/rebellion, and it was my father who now seemed distant. In particular I felt that he wasn't pleased with my writing. Yet, as I began to be published, that's who I was, and how I identified myself.

Still, we got on. He seemed to enjoy my company. We spent holidays together, and he helped me with a hundred house repairs. But he never mentioned the books I wrote.

Then he was ill. Then he was dying. Then I was sitting by his hospital bed, seeking the last approval, seeking the last blessing.

I brought my new books to the hospital room. I brought him stories of what I was doing. I said the words "I love you," and punctuated them with my tears. When he returned my declaration of love, I wanted to ask him if he also loved my books, if he also loved the writer I had become. I never did. Words seemed inadequate. What did "I love you" mean when the words were so expected? What did they mean when they echoed from antiseptic hospital walls but missed the uneasy contours of our relationship?

Sitting in my father's empty house after his death was hard. There were a thousand reminders of special moments gone by. The old cowboy belt he let me play with as a child but would never give me. The New Testament he had given me when, on my 17th birthday, I had joined the army. But it was his papers that fascinated me most. As I went through them I was shocked. I looked at them over and over, turning them in my hands, wondering why I had never guessed his secret before.

I remembered him coming to my house, asking me to read some document to him, saying that he had misplaced his glasses. I recalled him sitting at a table asking me to check if an insurance form was "filled out right" or if he had "signed in all the right places." My father couldn't read well enough to handle my books.

When I was a child my father talked to me, told me absurdly wonderful stories. It was these stories that allowed me to release the balloon of my imagination, and to let it soar. It was his stories, and those of my grandfather, that gave me permission to tell stories myself, to think it was the thing I wanted to do. I was allowed to take the world of the imagination and make it my own. It was my mother, reading her magazines, that furthered that imagination, gave it order, defined it more in words than pictures.

Herbert and Florence Dean were bridges I have crossed over. Bridges from the harder time they knew to the better time they did not know. They were willing to take me to the shores they weren't able to manage themselves, and bid me Godspeed.

I wish I had known my father couldn't read while he was alive. I would have told him my stories. I would have *read* to him the stories I had written, the same stories that he had once told me. But those times have passed and I'll take from them, and from what I have learned from them. That I, too, have stories to pass on and advice to give and a critical eye grounded in my own time and space.

My youngest boy was going for an interview recently. He's quite the young man now and fairly sure of himself. Despite my best intentions not to, I gave him all the advice I had promised myself I would withhold. "I think you're getting old," he said smiling. "You're sounding a lot like Grandpa."

It was one of the nicest things he's ever said to me. ■

Sunrise Sunset

by Jeanne Moutoussamy-Ashe

January 5th, 1922

The sun rises and the sun sets on daddy

May 6, 1995

The Gift

by Nikki Grimes
illustration by E. B. Lewis

I t's funny what you remember about a person, what images come to mind. I see my father's feet encased in whispers. He called them penny loafers, but I knew better. No shoe could give him the quiet power to steal into a room or up the stairs or down a glass-strewn city street without ever being heard, the way his penny loafers did.

James Grimes was of average height and slim, a soft-spoken man, often wrapped in silence. But he was intense. Energy emanated from his black skin like heat waves rising from hot tar on a city street in August. The passion in him might well have been the sublimated anger of a disenfranchised Black man living in America. Fortunately for his friends and family, Daddy's passion–most of it, anyway–stemmed from a rare zest for life, and a love of all things beautiful.

My father took great pleasure in, and felt enormous responsibility for, exposing my sister and me to the world of art. One might say that he dressed for the part, too, given as he was to wearing French berets, sports coats, loose-fitting slacks–and, of course, the requisite Italian leather loafers. This was his uniform, and I was happy to be seen with him in it, whether we went to a gallery showing of Tom Feelings and Leo Carty or to the cinema to view *Black Orpheus*, or to the theater to see *Les Ballets Africains*.

The world of dance was glorious to me, as were the worlds of visual art and literature and music. Thanks to my father, I learned to appreciate them all. But his most personal gift to me was the sharing of his passion for music, for he, himself, was a musician.

My father played the violin.

I never thought to ask how he came by his skill, nor did I ask where or when or from whom he'd learned musical notation. The music was simply always *there*. I took it for granted that he composed concertos, that his violin appeared to be a natural appendage. The man and the music were all of a piece in my mind, and I found it rather strange that other people considered my father's classical bent peculiar. Years later, of course, I realized how few Blacks of his generation were classical musicians.

Les Ballets Africains

You couldn't tell me nothin'
all decked out
in a brand new prissy smile
and fancy dress
clinging to Daddy's arm
his little lady off to see
Les Ballets Africains.
My imitation nonchalance
never made it much beyond
the dimming of
the lights in the theatre
Neither the
ebony-limbed women leaping
across the stage nor the
profusion
of kente, beads, and feathered
masks escaped my teenage
fascination.
Lost in meditation
I listened to the bare-chested
drummers muscle out
a message anyone
could understand
it seemed
to me.
"Come! Come!"
said the drumbeat
"Join us as we
worship through the dance."

In another sense, though, I found the delicate beauty, the tenderness, the very *fact* of my father's music miraculous. Many of my early years were spent in tenements and rail-road flats in Harlem and Brooklyn, and most of the sounds that reverberated through those mean streets were anything but lovely. The blare of jukebox music from the corner bar and grill was fairly tolerable. Not so the shrill sirens of ambulances and police cars speeding by at all hours of the night, or the frequent explosion of whiskey bottles against the sidewalk, or the crash of garbage cans in the alley; or the angry cussin' and screamin' of men and women facing-off next door, or across the hall. (*Man, don't you make me come over there and kick yo' Black–*). And let's not forget the sound of gun shots.

The noises inside the apartment were not much better: the clang and whistle of radiator pipes in winter, the scratch of mammoth roaches scuttling across the floor, and the skitter of sharp-toothed, long-tailed rats that (you hoped) were trapped inside the wall.

Magically, in and through it all, I remember the impossibly enchanting strains of my father's violin.

But where did it come from, all that hushed beauty? How was it possible to create musical passages so unutterably soothing, and melodious, while walled in by so much noise? I couldn't help but wonder.

The answer, of course, was that the music came from within. My father had, by God's grace, learned to filter the noxious noises of the world, to refine them in the furnace of his own emotions, and then shape them into delicate strands of sound that hit the air as softly as his leather loafers hit the pavement. What's more, he managed to convince me–as much by deed as word, I think–that, through my poetry, I could learn to do the same. My stubborn attempts, today, to create literature worthy to be so called, owes much to his influence.

How often my father spoke to me of the wonder and power of art! Sadly, he was never able to pursue his own art full time, as I now do. He earned his bread and meat as a buyer for a discount clothing factory outlet, while his music–his true calling–was relegated to the status of a glorified hobby. He was forced to squeeze in hours of practice and play where he could, in the evenings and on weekends. Still, he made the best of it.

My guess is that he put in one or two hours of play each night. I say "guess" because I wasn't around to witness many practice sessions. My parents divorced before I was six years old.

I saw my father on weekends, mostly, but my visits with him were memorable, punctuated as they were by the private "concerts" he would give me at my urging. (*Oh, Daddy, please, pretty please play something for me!* I'd beg. And, smiling, he'd always comply. I see him now, raising his violin to his chin, closing his eyes and caressing the violin strings until they tremble with sweet sound.)

The greatest treat was when he set one of my poems to music, sometimes on the spot! Little wonder that, for me, music and poetry are forever linked.

Daddy ate, drank, and breathed music. Bach. Beethoven. Dvorak. Joplin. Ellington. Max Roach. Miriam Makeba. Miles. He loved it all. He went to live concerts when he could, and listened to recordings on his suped-up stereo when he could not. Most important, whenever the opportunity presented itself, he played.

"Your father loved to play Handel's *Messiah*," my mother told me years after he died. "Every Christmas, he'd drive all over town, sitting in with any orchestra that could use an extra violin. Sometimes he'd drive as far as Jersey." Odd that I never knew about that. But one thing I did know: he dreamed of playing at Carnegie Hall.

Daddy spoke of this dream often, and always with a faraway look in his eyes. I'm not sure how he pulled it off, but before he died, my father and a group of players he routinely jammed with gave a performance in one of Carnegie's small recital halls. I can't recall the specific piece he played to mark the occasion, only that his smile was the most luminous I'd ever seen him wear.

I'm grateful that he grasped every opportunity to share his music with his friends and family, because he died in a car crash before the age of 45. What if, like many people I know, he had thought to postpone pursuing his music until retirement? His gift might well have been wasted.

But Daddy didn't believe in wasting time. Or talent. Or love. He understood the preciousness of each, and spent them all. And in the spending, he taught me this: Walk softly. Love life. Dream. Find a little beauty. Create a little more. Most important, share your treasures while you may. ∎

Definition

Love is not the only face

a poem wears

a poem can be shaped to cry

know rage, a tear

can stomp or twirl mixed

rhythms

a poem is munitions dump

is lance

is arrow

a poem is a veto

a short straw for the war

a monument to martyr

a tribute to scarred knee'd

straight back'd

* Black women*

a poem is

an act

or more.

No less

Black Woman

by Tom Feelings

I thought that it was because I had lived and traveled in Africa I was able to see clearly the great quality of power, openness, and balance that so struck me in Black women . . . but when I came back to America and looked into the face of my mother I saw it all there, too–for the first time. Then I realized it had always been there, in her eyes and in my grandmother's eyes.

It had only been clouded by my experience of living in America.

Finally, I understood that Africa's beauty, strength, and dignity are wherever the Black woman is.

"Home"
by Gwendolyn Brooks

Home ... always warmly awaited me. Welcoming, enveloping. Home meant a quick-walking, careful, Duty-Loving mother, who played the piano, made fudge, made cocoa and prune whip and apricot pie, drew tidy cows and trees and expert houses with chimneys and chimney smoke, who helped her children with arithmetic homework, and who sang in a high soprano:

> "Brighten the corner where you are!—
> Br-rrr-righten the corner where you are!—
> Some one far from harbor you may guide
> across the bar—
> Brigh-TEN the cor-nerr—
> where
> you
> are."

Home meant my father, with kind eyes, songs, and tense recitations for my brother and myself. A favorite of his, a wonderful poem about a pie-making lady. Along had come a man, weary, worn, to beg of the lady a pie. Those already baked, she informed him, were too large for the likes of him. She said she would bake another. It, too, was "large." And the next was large. And the next, and the next. Finally the traveler, completely out of patience, berated her and exclaimed that henceforth she should draw her own sustenance from the bark of trees. And she became, *mirabile dictu*, a woodpecker and flew off. We never tired of that. My father seemed to Gwendolyn and Raymond a figure of power. He had those rich Artistic Abilities, but he had more. He could fix anything that broke or stopped. He could build long-lasting fires in the ancient furnace below. He could paint the house, inside and out, and could whitewash the basement. He could spread the American Flag in wide loud magic across the front of our house on the Fourth of July and Decoration Day. He could chuckle. No one has ever had, no one will ever have, a chuckle exactly like my father's. It was gentle, it was warmly happy, it was heavyish but not hard. It was secure, and seemed to us an assistant to the Power that registered with his children. My father, too, was almost our family doctor. We had Dr. Carter, of course, precise and semi-twinkly and effective—but it was not always necessary to call him. My father had wanted to be a doctor. Thwarted, he read every "doctor book" (and he remembered much from a black tradition) he could reach, learning fine secrets and curing us with steams, and fruit compotes, and dexterous rubs, and, above all, with bedside compassion. "Well, let's see now. This salve will take care of that bruise! Now, we're going to be all right." In illness there was an advantage: the invalid was royalty for the run of the seizure.

And of course my father furnished All the Money. The "all" was inadequate, felt Keziah Wims Brooks: could he not leave the McKinley Music Publishing Company, which was paying him about twenty-five dollars a week (from thirty to thirty-five when he worked overtime)? Uncle Paul, her sister Gertrude's husband, worked at City Hall—had a "snap" job—made *fifty* dollars a week....True, during the bad times, during the Depression, when McKinley, itself stricken, could pay my father only in part—sometimes eighteen dollars, sometimes ten dollars—our family ate beans. But children dread, often above all else, dissension in the house, and we would have been quite content to entertain a beany diet every day, if necessary, and *not* live in Lilydale, as did bungalow-owning Aunt Gertrude and Uncle Paul, if only there could be, continuously, the almost musical Peace that we had most of the time.

Home. Checker games. Dominoes. Radio (Jack Benny, Ben Bernie, and Kate Smith; "Amos and Andy"; Major Bowes' "Amateur Hour"; Wayne King, the Waltz King; and "Ladies and Gentlemen: Ea-sy Aces")....■

Mom, Dad, Family, and Me

an interview with Brian Pinkney

photographs by Myles Pinkney

When I first started going around looking for work I had two thoughts at the same time. One, I knew that my parents had a lot of connections, that they could offer me a lot of help in terms of places to go to show my work. But there was a part of me that wanted to do it all by myself. So sometimes when I'd go to see publishers I wouldn't give them my true name. Then other times, I would use the contacts my mother had given me. She knew a lot of different publishers because at one time she was my father's agent. After a while it just kind of came together. Basically I acknowledge and am proud that I have Gloria and Jerry Pinkney as my mom and dad.

Your father has been a strong mentor and father figure for a number of young Black illustrators, giving generously of his time and advice. Has it been difficult sharing him with so many others?

I think I've always gotten one hundred percent from both my parents. Having had four children who were very close in age, my parents did a very good job of making sure that we all got what we needed. Today, my father gives me one hundred percent of encouragement and validation.

Have books always been important to you?

As a child, I read a lot of the books my father had illustrated. I modeled for many of them as well. I also spent time in the library. And the books I took out from the library were mostly how-to or arts and craft type books. I was very involved in making my own toys. I used pipe cleaners and corks, and paper towel rolls and things, and I liked building things like hydrofoils.

Who were some of your favorite authors and illustrators when you were growing up?

My father was number one because his were the first books I saw. I remember looking at a lot of books when I was young, but I don't remember paying attention to who the authors and illustrators were. I know I liked Maurice Sendak. I remember admiring Tom Feelings's and Muriel Feelings's books also. And I liked the character Curious George.

Why did you decide to become an illustrator, particularly one of children's books? Did you pursue it, or did it pursue you?

I always enjoyed drawing and painting but what inspired me the most was my father. I knew I wanted to be just like him when I grew up. I loved music, too, but it was really the art that I could see myself making a living doing. I realized at a young age that a person could make a living as an artist; it's something I took for granted. Once I got out of school I really pursued a career in the industry. I realized that I had to spend a lot of time hitting the pavement, going to art directors, getting interviews with publishers, and setting up my portfolio.

My parents were very encouraging. They had given me a lot of validation when I was growing up. When I was making pictures and building things, I just saw it as a form of play. I was drawing because it was fun. It was my mother who usually found me in the corner of my room drawing or building something. She would always say, "Wow, that's beautiful. Go show it to your father." And because my father had a studio in the house, I would go up and show him what I had done. Later, when Mom saw that I was very serious about art she converted a walk-in closet into a studio for me. I think for my 10th birthday I got a drafting table–a miniature one just like the one Dad used–paint sets, paint brushes, and I set up my own little studio. I even had a little taboret where I kept all my paint supplies.

What was the first book you illustrated?

The Storyteller. It was published by Songhay Press, a small independent company in Philadelphia. It was an assignment I got my senior year in college. The author, who's also the publisher, was looking for an artist for a story he had written. He looked at a few portfolios at the University of the Arts in Philadelphia (formerly Philadelphia College of Art), where I was getting my under-

graduate degree, and he decided on me. It was done in dark pencil drawings; it printed in black and white.

At the start of your career were you intimidated by the success your father and mother had achieved?

I wasn't intimidated by their success. Having grown up with them, it was just a part of my life. If anything, it gave me a lot of confidence that this was something that I could do. When I first started going around looking for work I had two thoughts at the same time. One, I knew that my parents had a lot of connections, that they could offer me a lot of help in terms of places to go to show my work. But there was a part of me that wanted to do it all by myself. So sometimes when I'd go to see publishers I wouldn't give them my true name. Then other times, I would use the contacts my mother had given me. She knew a lot of different publishers because at one time she was my father's agent. After a while it just kind of came together. Basically I acknowledge and am proud that I have Gloria and Jerry Pinkney as my mom and dad.

The scratchboard technique has become almost a signature for you. It is very graphic, textured, and has an almost sculptural feel. How did that style evolve?

When I was much younger, many of the drawings that I really admired were from the old pulp comic books from the nineteen thirties and forties. I had a book that had lots of samples of that style. The drawings were usually done in black and white. At the time I was working in pen and ink a lot and

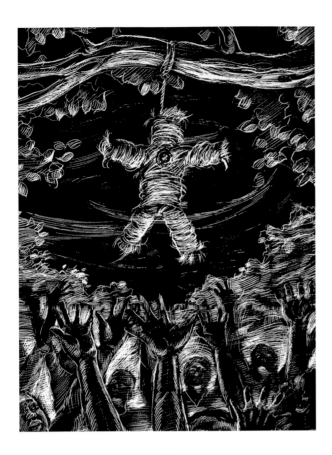

around with different techniques. And one of the techniques was scratchboard. He gave me this little piece of scratchboard and I did a little drawing. It felt so natural that I wanted to do all my illustrations that way. From that point on, I went to all of my publishers and said, "This is how I want to illustrate the rest of my books." I don't know where the style is eventually going, but at the moment I really enjoy working this way.

I think the sculptural way that I see images probably came from my desire to build things when I was younger. When I illustrate, I like to get the image as three dimensional as possible. Scratchboard helps me achieve this effect.

I thought that those illustrations were in pen and ink because they were black and white. Looking back now, I realize that many of the illustrations were actually done in scratchboard, a technique where a white board is covered with black ink that is then scratched away with a sharp tool. I remember that these drawings were moody and some were very dark. I have always been trying to achieve that effect in my work.

I also spent a lot of time taking etching and lithography classes. Etching is a print-making technique very much like scratchboard. In it you scratch your drawings onto a zinc plate and then print onto paper. When I was getting my master's degree from the School of Visual Arts one of my teachers suggested that we play

You probably get a number of inquiries from publishers who want you to illustrate stories. How do you decide what manuscripts you will illustrate?

I am selective in terms of the manuscripts that I choose to illustrate. How I decide what I am going to illustrate usually depends on what grabs me. I don't know ahead of time what type of subject matter I want to illustrate. I do know I'm focusing on African-American subject matter because it feels closest to me and we really need these types of books out there. I need to be personally drawn into the story. It may just be me identifying with the character, or it may be an image that I really want to draw. If I read a story over a few times and it seems to get deeper and deeper for me and I see the images evolving, I usually decide I'm going to illustrate it.

Your brother Myles is a photographer. Is creativity in your genes?

Well, I don't really know too much about genetics, but I do know that everyone in my family is very creative. My other brother, Scott, is an art director, a vice president of an advertising agency, and a graphic designer. My sister, Troy, is Director of Child Life at Albert Einstein Hospital. She uses art therapy and is very creative in her own right. Most of my nieces and nephews show a real interest in drawing and in the arts in general. Maybe it is genetic. Or maybe it's that we all were very much encouraged to make pictures and to draw and to express ourselves in different creative ways. It's probably a combination of the two.

Your wife, Andrea, is a writer and editor. Would you describe how you work together?

First of all, our schedules are very different. I'm very much of a night person and Andrea is more of a morning person. So our days don't cross all that much in terms of working together except maybe on the weekends.

Usually we want to do a project that we're both very much interested in. For example, we both came up with the idea of doing a book on choreographer/dancer Alvin Ailey. It was the same thing with *Seven Candles for Kwanzaa*. Most times, Andrea starts writing the story and when she gets to a point where she maybe feels stuck, I'll read it. At that point, we handle it like a meeting. We sit down at the dining room table and discuss it. She has one request, which is that when I make my comments I start off by saying, "Honey, you're off to a great start!" Starting off with a positive comment like that is very good for our marriage. It usually breaks the ice and then I can get to more critical things that I may want to say about the manuscript. Likewise, when I'm working on the images, I'll do the dummy book. Then she will look at it and make suggestions or comments. I really value Andrea's critiques and her opinion. She's very good at seeing things that I can't see.

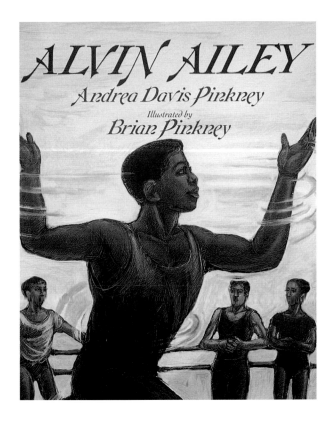

Do you see any parallels between your parents' teamwork and that of you and your wife?

I do see a parallel. I don't get to see my parents' process, how they work daily together, as much as I used to, but I do know that they are very courteous to each other, and that is one of the things that Andrea and I try hard to do. I know that my father really values my mother's opinions of his artwork, and I know she values his opinions of her work. We spend a lot of time as a family looking at each other's work. I show my sketches and finishes to my father a lot, and he shows me the things he's working on. I often talk on the phone with my mother and she'll often read me her works in progress.

What are some of your future plans?

To continue collaborating with Andrea, for one. We have some other book projects that we're working on together. I'm also interested in illustrating other types of stories that are very different than Andrea writes. And I'm working on my own story ideas, too. ■

RINNNG

Tuesday (Chattanooga, TN)

by Angela Johnson
illustration by Javaka Steptoe

Washed our clothes at the laundromat next door
from the bakery–where everything smelled of bread and
fabric softener

She'd strip the baby down to his diaper and let him crawl
underneath the tables, brown and glowing and only two teeth,
and me . . .

'Cause it must be Tuesday
when Mama would put everything in an old army duffel
that Grandma bought her when she left . . .

Grabbed us and locked the door, down the stairs,
into the heat and down the street.
–and it's our best place.

It must be Tuesday 'cause a machine she'd just filled with clothes
doesn't work, and she smiled at me . . .

Then home, and she misses the last phone ring
and drops the baby on the couch
Three overdue bills and no milk while we crawl over her
and she's warm.
–And it's alright for a Tuesday.

Undue Burden

by Mildred Pitts Walter
photograph by Chester Higgins, Jr.

It was a warm windy day. The sheets, towels, and shirts on our clothesline made a popping noise, sending moisture into the air to help build the soft white clouds racing with the wind. Just as Mama started the fire in the small metal furnace to heat irons for pressing clothes, a convertible car sped up to our house in a cloud of dust.

Mama frowned. What does she want now? Then with a slight smile, she quickly went to meet Mrs. Sailor, one of the women for whom she worked.

Mama was a midwife and hairdresser by trade, but during those years people had little money to pay for those services. In the 1930s times were tough. Many men left home looking for work, leaving women to keep families together. When Papa left, Mama joined a host of other Black women who did day work and laundry for White women.

Wages were low in our small Louisiana town. For six days of cleaning and cooking, most women did well to make five dollars. Compared to others, Mrs. Sailor paid well–a dollar for only one day. But that was not much for what Mrs. Sailor received beyond a clean house. Often, she was heard to say, "Marie, you're like one in the family."

Mrs. Sailor felt free to come to our house whenever there was trouble in hers. And there was trouble a plenty. Her husband was a hot-tempered man who abused her and their two sons–one eight and one six. Sometimes she rushed to Mama with blackened eyes and other bruises.

She never came into our house, and Mama never got into her car. Mama leaned into the window and listened to tearful talk. Sometimes Mrs. Sailor got out of her car, reached up and put her arms around Mama's neck, and sobbed aloud.

Mrs. Sailor was much younger than Mama. Her thick red hair, not covered with a scarf that day, was wind-blown, and her exposed, ruddy cheeks were dry except for the tears that slowly crept down and around her nose.

She talked to Mama briefly.

Mama hurriedly dressed and left with her.

The schedule for people's laundry was right on time, but now . . . what was the urgency? And why didn't Mama say she couldn't go?

The day went by. My sisters started the ironing, hoping that Mama would soon return and supervise their work. Noon came. No Mama. Five o'clock. No Mama. It was time to worry. Finally, she came. What had taken her so long?

She told us that Mrs. Sailor had been almost hysterical with worry. Had to go to bed. And every time Mama got ready to leave, Mrs. Sailor insisted that she stay with her. Mister Sailor was there, too. He was restless. He smelled of alcohol and smoked one cigarette after another. At first Mama thought Mrs. Sailor might have done something to upset him, and, uneasy, she told Mrs. Sailor that she didn't want to get involved in their problems. She had to go home–there was

laundry to do. Mrs. Sailor insisted that she had done nothing to upset him. She continued to cry and plead not to be left alone.

Finally, much later, on the way home in the car, even though they were alone, Mrs. Sailor began whispering.

Before dawn, her husband was driving home and hit something with his car. He didn't stop. Around five that morning, he had called the garage owner, and asked him to send Tom, a young Black man who worked in the garage, to pick up his car to repair a leaking hose. He needed the car back by eight. Tom picked up the car around five thirty.

Some time after six that morning the body of the mayor of the town was discovered on a side street. At the garage, the mechanic found no leaking hose, but there were dents in the left fender. After a closer look the owner of the garage found a pipe, still filled with tobacco, lodged into the bumper. It was the mayor's pipe. He called the police.

The police went immediately to question Mister Sailor about his car. Mister Sailor said he knew nothing about an accident. It was after the police left that Mrs. Sailor came for Mama.

When the tears started to flow again, she asked Mama, "What can we do?" Mama couldn't tell her what to do. And Mama wondered why was Mrs. Sailor telling all of that?

We listened in silence. Mama, though exhausted, went to work on the ironing board. She closed into herself and all evening said nothing more. We left her to her burdened thoughts.

The next day we learned that Tom, who was well known, and well liked, had been arrested, accused of the hit-and-run death of Mayor Doss.

It was not until many years later that I fully understood it all.

Surely Mama knew that as it was with Tom, so could it be with her son. How she must have longed to cry out Tom's innocence. But who would have believed her? And who would have protected her witnessing? People had lost their lives for telling *less* than what she knew.

How had Mama, within the ring of that terrible truth, been able to keep her sanity, go on with her life?

What was it that kept her whole? Faith in God? Love for her family? Her fierce protection of us, especially our brother? *I don't know.*

I only know that chained in powerlessness she stayed the course, raised her family, and contributed to the community.

For that I give her praise. ■

What It Means to Be My Father's Son

by Bakari Kitwana
sculpture by Tina Allen

Watching my father day in and day out for the last four years of his life, which he lived paralyzed from the neck down, placed a heavy burden on my teenaged mind. How could I share the things that teenage males share with their fathers? With both my brothers away at college and my father bouncing around from hospital to hospital, from specialist to specialist, I was the only male at home with my mother and four sisters. But by no means was I "the man of the house": neither my father nor my mother would ever let me be so presumptuous as to think that at the age of 14 I knew what it meant to be a man. And after that decisive crippling auto accident, after touching hands that my father could not feel, after seeing tubes in his nose, mouth, and elsewhere, I discovered very early that life was not to be taken lightly.

My father's immobility did not impede his invigorating spiritual energy. Neither did it stop him from teaching in words and example what it meant to be a man, a son, a father, a husband, a friend, or what it means to be Black. It did not stop him from teaching me integrity, honesty, dignity, self-respect, pride, and the importance of family, spirituality, community, friendship, love, and responsibility. He made a point of emphasizing that life is full of good and bad times. "Store up the good memories," he once said, "for they become your house of refuge in trying times."

Tina Allen
Proud Father and Son
private collection

I remember family trips to Weeksville, North Carolina, every summer to visit my grandparents. My father, Sam Dance–son of Ida Dance and Willy Spellman, born September 22, 1930, named for his maternal great-grandfather, Sam Bailey, a former enslaved African–married at 20 and moved to Long Island, New York, in the summer of 1955. My father's father died as a young man of tuberculosis in Weeksville during the summer of 1934 at the age of 24. At the time, my father was four years old. He spoke rarely of his childhood years except for a few incidentals–long walks, driving tractors, placing newspapers on the walls to keep out the winter's cold.

The last time I saw my father alive I kissed him good-bye. I had just completed my first semester of my freshman year of college. (I had decided that I was grown-up enough to kiss my father again.) I will never forget that good-bye. I have relived it for more than a dozen Christmases and Thanksgivings and New Years and September 22nds and many times in between.

I can remember when I first discovered that my father could not read. We were headed south in the family car to North Carolina. It was night time. The sound of passing cars had become as routine as the soothing hum of the engine. My mother read the road signs aloud to my father and pointed the way. A wrong turn more than once led to frustration. It was the sound of frustra-tion in my father's voice that woke me from my cozy car ride slumber. He had left school at the age of 10 to go to work to help his mother. At age 50 he returned to school and finally learned to read and write. And I remember how my younger sister learned to read. She was not quite four years old, not yet ready for school, when Daddy took out the time to teach her in a few weeks what his life's path kept from him for more than 40 years.

I often gaze into old photos of my parents together. Most of these photos are older than I, and they are tired from the years, and the wear and tear of touch. Yet, what remains intact is my parents' happiness, love and the beauty of life. When my father passed, my mother never let us forget that he would always be a part of our lives.

I never saw my father high, never saw him drunk, never heard him curse, never knew him to hit my mother, never saw my father interact with anyone in a manner that was other than honorable and respectful. Clean. Neat. Clean-shaven. Shined shoes. Well-dressed. My father was not perfect, but a sense of the sacred, a respect for creation, governed his movement in the world.

I often return home for holidays and family gatherings. Over the years a lot has changed. A modern linoleum rug covers bathroom floors that my father once created one tile at a time . . . bedroom walls he

once painted sky blue have been repainted various shades of a darker blue . . . the place that was once his sick room, the space where he took his last breath, has become a family room. But it is still the home that my mother and father built together. The flowers he planted long ago continue to bloom each spring. And I am reminded of what it means to build a home, to be a father and a husband, of what it means to be my father's son. ∎

A Personal Journey
Race, Rage, and Intellectual Development
by *Haki R. Madhubuti*
photographs by *Ron Ceasar*

I grew up on the Lower East Side of Detroit and West Side of Chicago in a family that lived too often from week to week. My mother, sister, and I represented the nucleus of our family. In 1943, my mother migrated from Little Rock, Arkansas, moving, as John O. Killens would say, "up-South" to Michigan. She came with my father, who stayed long enough to father my sister, who is a year and a half younger than I. I was born in 1942.

Those years, the 1940s and 1950s, were not kind to us, and my father wandered in and out of our lives from the day we hit Detroit. My mother, alone with two children and no skills, ended up working as a janitor in an apartment building owned by a Negro preacher/undertaker. My earliest memory is of her cleaning that three-story, 16-unit building each day, carrying garbage cans on her back to the alley once a week. Seldom did I see her without a broom, mop, or wash cloth in her hands. By this time, I was eight years old, and my sister was seven. We helped as much as possible because we knew that staying in our basement apartment depended upon our keeping the building clean.
I did not know then that our housing also depended upon my mother's sexual involvement with the Negro building owner. These encounters took place when we were at school or while we were asleep. My mother began to trade her body quite early in order for us to live . . .

With no family in Detroit and left to her own limited re-sources, my mother sought to survive with her children in a way that would have the least possible negative impact on us. However, due to the violent nature of her relationship with the landlord, we stayed in our Lower East Side apartment only until she was able to find work less threatening and taxing on her physically and psychologically. At least that is what my sister and I thought. What I've failed to tell you about my mother is that she was probably one of the most beautiful women in the world. I've seen her beauty not only stop traffic but compel men to literally get out of their cars to introduce themselves to her. Her beauty, which was both physical and internal, was something that the few women she associated with could not handle. Women would stare at her with dropped mouths. Her beauty would ultimately place her in an environment that would destroy her.

My mother's next job was that of a barmaid. She started serving drinks at one of the newest and classiest locations in Detroit, Sonny Wilson's. Along with this job came the slow but destructive habit of alcohol consumption. Also, she began to run in very fast company. She was named Miss Barmaid of 1951, carrying with that title all of the superficiality and glitter of the Negro entertainment world at that time. To cut to the bone of all of this is to note rather emphatically that my family's condition of poverty drove my mother into a culture that dictated both her destruction and great misery for my sister and me. By the time I was 13, my mother was a confirmed alcoholic and was fast losing her health. When I turned 15, she had moved to hard drugs and was not functional most of the time.

My sister, who had just turned 14, announced to us that she was pregnant. This was in the late 1950s and pregnancy out of wedlock was not a common or acceptable occurrence. I went out looking for the man who had impregnated her. He was a local gang leader, 21 years old, who had as much potential as a husband or father as I did at 15. After briefly talking to him about my sister's condition and getting virtually nowhere, I did what most "men" did in similar situations at that time: I hit him.

And he, in a rather surgical fashion, responded by literally "kicking my ass." After reporting this to my mother, she, in a drunken stupor, gave me another whipping for getting whipped.

Shortly after that incident, my mother's need for alcohol and drugs increased. She prostituted herself to feed her habit. Many nights I searched Detroit's transient hotels looking for her. Needless to say, I had grown up rather quickly and felt that there was no hope for me or my sister. Just before I turned 16, my mother overdosed on drugs and died. She had been physically and sexually abused by someone so badly that we were not able to view her body at her funeral . . .

I could not cry at my mother's funeral. My heart was cold and my mind was psychologically tired. I felt a quiet feeling of relief and release at her death, but also an underlying tone of guilt. At 16, I felt that I had not done enough to save my mother. However, it was clear to me that her final days had been filled with long hours of tragic suffering over which she had no control. All I could do was watch in confused pain, hostility, anger, resentment, and rage.

At first, I could not understand my anger. Why did she have to die so young and so viciously? Why were my sister, her baby, and I alone without help or hope? Why were we so poor? It seemed that my life was one big fight. There was no escape from problems and very little peace. And I guess my mother's death brought a moment of peace. The fight to survive remained uppermost in my mind. Yet it seemed I was being torn apart from the inside. A part of my own fear was connected to how my sister and I were going to survive. I had seen and been a part of too much destruction and death in my young life. I knew that the only person who really cared about our future was me, and that was not enough.

I had few friends, partially because of my economic condition; I had little time to play because I had to work. Also, my social skills were not the best and the path of the loner best suited me at that time. I did not realize then that solitary existence was to eventually save my life.

Color in America

A part of the problem that my mother, sister, and I faced in America was that our skin color was neither black nor white, but yellow! . . .

It was [my mother's] beauty, illuminated by very light skin color, that attracted the darkest of Black men and, of those I remember, the most abusive of Black men. They seemed to be steaming in anger, hatred, and internal rage. It seems as though by being with her, they were as close to White women as was allowed at that time. And their often intense love/hate relationship with her was only a mirror of the fight they were having daily with themselves and the White world. They could not touch or physically retaliate against White people, but my mother was there for many of them to play out their deepest hurt in their "loving" and abusive treatment of her. I was not to understand, until much later, the deep color-rage that plagued them and that lay at the surface of my own reality.

Being a "yellow nigger" in urban America was like walking on roasted toothpicks hanging from the mouths of brothers who did not like the taste of wood or understand themselves. Many of the Black men who populated my early life used self-defacing language 24 hours a day. The operative words used constantly were *nigger* and *mothaf———*. We had not only been seasoned to dislike or hate the "us" in us, but also adopted the language of self-abuse and self-hatred. I learned early to walk the fine line between Black and White. I began to understand the anger, hatred, and rage in me by studying Black literature and Black music.

What Saved Me?

At 13, my mother asked me to go to the Detroit Public Library to check out a book for her. The title of the book was *Black Boy*. . . . I refused to go because I didn't want to go anywhere asking for anything Black. The self-hatred that occupied my mind, body, and soul simply prohibited me from going to a White library in 1955 to request from a White librarian a book by a Black author, especially with

Black in the title. . . . However, *Black Boy* had somehow attached itself to my mother's mind and would not let go. I went to the library, found the book on the shelf myself, put it to my chest, found an unpeopled spot, and began to read the book that would profoundly alter my life.

For the first time in my life, I was reading words developed into ideas that were not insulting to my own personhood. Richard Wright's experiences were mine even though we were separated by geography. I read close to half of the book before the library closed. I checked *Black Boy* out, hurried home, went into my room I shared with my sister, and read for the rest of the night. Upon completing *Black Boy* the next morning, I was somehow a different type of questioner in school and at home. I had not totally changed, but the foundation had been planted. Deeply. I became more concerned about the shape of things around me. I also read Wright's *Native Son*, *Uncle Tom's Children*, and *12 Million Black Voices*. Richard Wright painted pictures with words that connected to the real me. I could relate to Bigger Thomas because his fears, doubts, and internal rage were the same that I experienced. Layers of ignorance were being removed by just opening my mind to a world that included me as a whole person. Wright entered my life at the right time.

After my mother's death, I took the Greyhound to Chicago, where I stayed with an aunt for a while, then rented a room at the Southside YMCA. I completed high school in Chicago and ended up in St. Louis, Missouri, where I joined the United States Army.

The military was the poor boy's employment. On the way to basic training at Fort Leonard Wood, Missouri, I was reading Paul Robeson's *Here I Stand*. When we arrived at boot camp, the White, middle-30ish drill sergeant ordered us off the bus. We were about two hundred men. Three Black men, including myself, and one hundred ninety-seven White men. The Black men had all joined voluntarily, but most of the White men were drafted. This was

1960, and the Army was practicing "integration."

As I stepped off the bus, the White drill sergeant sighted Paul Robeson's face on my book and snatched it from my hand. He pulled me out of line and barked into my face, "What's your Negro mind doing reading this Black communist?" Of course, many thoughts ran through my head as potential responses to his question. This was the first time I had heard a double negative used so creatively. The drill sergeant ordered all of us up against the bus and commenced to tear pages from the book, giving a page to each recruit, and telling the recruits to use the pages for toilet paper. By this time, I was questioning my own sanity about joining the military and examining my options.

Luckily, I was also reading John O. Killens's, *And Then We Heard the Thunder*, a powerful and telling book about Black men in Europe's War on the World Number Two (commonly referred to as World War II). What I learned from Killens was the importance of using one's time wisely and never to speak from the top of one's head in anger when outnumbered. As I stood, lips closed, cold and shaking with fear, anger, and loneliness–while the sergeant destroyed my copy of Robeson's work–I decided four things that would stay with me for the rest of my life:

1. I would never, never again apologize for being Black. I am who I am, I realized then, and if Black literature has taught me anything, it clarified for me that I was a man of African descent in America serving time in the United States Army rather than the United States prison system.

2. I would never again put myself in a cultural or intellectual setting where people outside of my culture or race would know more about me than I knew about myself. . . .

3. I was in the United States Army because I was Black, poor, and ignorant of the forces that controlled my life and the lives of other men–Black and White–with whom I was to train. These forces were racial, economic, and political,

and I needed accurate information on all of them. While many of the other brothers in my platoon searched for fun, I visited the libraries. Few could understand why I chose to be alone with books. The reason was that I found new friends, uncritical friends in the literature. I was a sponge. Reading became as important as water and food.

4. If *ideas* were that powerful and could cause such a reaction, then I was going to get into the *idea* business. For that drill sergeant to act so violently against a book that contained ideas that he probably did not even understand was frightening. He was reacting to the image and idea of Paul Robeson that had been created by monied, political, and mass media White power brokers.

From that day on, I have been on a mission to understand the world and to be among the progressive men who want to change it for the benefit of the majority who occupy it. ■

Jurdine, Jurdine

by Wade Hudson

Mansfield, Louisiana, the place where I was born and raised, is a rural town nestled in the north western part of the state. It looks much the same as it did 30 years ago. There are very few new buildings. Most of the downtown structures are small and old: some look as if they will collapse at any time. Although some streets have been upgraded, they are still quite narrow. The pace of life is still painfully slow for those of us who are accustomed to big-city living. Most people speak to everyone and are eager to engage in conversation.

When I was growing up, Mansfield had to be as segregated a town as any place in the United States. "Colored" and "White Only" signs were posted everywhere. I saw very few Whites on a regular basis, other than insurance people and other salesmen pushing their products. Sometimes, my brother Willie and I would cross the invisible line that divided the town to mow lawns and we would encounter several Whites then or when we went with our parents downtown to shop.

The Whites wielded all the political and economic power in Mansfield, and controlled virtually everything else. Blacks were conditioned to stay in their place. It was not uncommon for a White man to shoot a Black person for the smallest offense. And often we were shot or jailed for offenses that were imaginary.

As a youngster, I would sit on the back porch steps of our house on Mary Street and write about all the wrongs I saw. I once wrote a letter to United States Attorney General Robert Kennedy explaining the plight of Blacks in Mansfield. I urged him to do something about the problems. He wrote back (or rather, his office did), telling me that he and his brother the President would do all they could to see to it that all Americans were treated equally.

Despite all the hell most White people put Black folks through, Mansfield was still a nurturing place. In the Black community, folks cared for each other and looked out for each other as best they could. And most pulled for each other to succeed. Our neighbors were like family. There were the Hendersons, the Lees, the Halls, the Blows, and Lela Johnson, who insisted we call her Grandma Lela. And, of course, there was our actual family, including our extended family. The entire community was like an omnipresent mother, caring for, nurturing, protecting, feeding, and scolding its young. Dad had been a laborer. Ma'Dear did domestic work when she wasn't having one of us. They worked hard and loved us even harder.

Eventually, everyone in my family—my siblings, my mother and my father, and me—moved away from Mansfield. Everyone except Jurdine, my oldest sister. She remained there with her husband and children.

Jurdine was six years older than I. I always felt that she thought it was an honor to look after me and my other sister and six brothers. Jurdine was a really generous, kind, and caring person. She loved life and she loved giving to others and watching them enjoy the gifts she had given. Every Christmas she would make my favorite pie (lemon meringue), cut a large slice, and place it on a plate. Then she would smile as she watched me devour it. In many ways she was like the mothering part of Mansfield, reaching out to embrace and shore up those with whom she came in contact.

And she had a hearty laugh, a southern laugh: full, vibrant, and jolly. And, my, how Jurdine *loved* to talk. Our family is nothing but talkers, and Jurdine was the greatest talker of us all, bound to speak three words

to every one word spoken by others and still tuck in a few laughs.

School work came easier for me than it did for her, and she was always so proud when I made the honor roll or was recognized for some other academic accomplishment. I can hear her now: "Brother, I sure felt good when I saw you walk up there to get that award. It was just like me getting it." And she meant every word.

Once, when I was in the first grade, I got into a fight with a set of twins. One of them hit me in the back of the head with a bottle. When Jurdine heard about it, she was furious. At the end of the school day she was waiting for the twins. I missed several days of school because of the injury. When I returned, everyone was talking about how my sister had beaten up the twins *and* their bigger sister and brother! That was Jurdine. My big sister.

Early on a Sunday morning in November 1995, my aunt Margaret called to tell us that Jurdine had been rushed to the hospital. Jurdine was in serious condition, Aunt Margaret said. She had suffered a massive heart attack and was in a coma.

The next morning I was on my way to Louisiana.

She was in a hospital in Shreveport, about 20 miles from Mansfield. When I first saw her lying there in that hospital bed with tubes and contraptions connected to all parts of her body, my legs nearly gave way. I closed my eyes and tried to swallow back the tears. Finally, I gathered myself and forced a smiled even though I knew she could not see me.

"Jurdine, Jurdine," I whispered softly.

She lay still. As I looked at her, I could hear my heart pounding. I thought, *It just doesn't seem real my big sister lying here like this . . . She should be at her house, cooking one of those cakes she enjoyed baking. She should be chatting with her neighbors . . . She shouldn't be here! Not here!*

"Jurdine. Jurdine." I called more loudly, though I didn't think she could hear me. "This is Brother. Jurdine, this is Brother. I'm here."

Suddenly, her body jerked and then began to tremble. It was as if she were exerting all the energy she could muster to rise up from that bed.

"I love you, Jurdine. You'll pull through this. With the help of the Lord, and all the love from your family, you'll pull through this."

She lay still again.

Her husband, John, stood a few feet behind me, not wanting to interfere with my chance to connect with my sister, knowing how close the two of us were.

I stayed in the hospital room with Jurdine and John for a while longer and then headed for the waiting room. Once in the hallway, I sobbed.

I spent as much time with my sister as the hospital would permit. During my visits I held her hand, rubbed her forehead, prayed, told her how much I loved her.

Each day she got a little better, finally regaining consciousness. By the fourth day, she was able to sit up in a chair for an hour or so. Many of the tubes were removed, but she still needed the respirator, which prevented her from talking, and I knew how difficult that must have been for her.

As each day passed, the doctors grew more optimistic about Jurdine's progress. Even though she could not talk, she could move her lips. "I love you, too," she mouthed many times.

We spent long moments holding hands and looking into each other's eyes. As our eyes locked, I sometimes wondered what she was thinking. Was she remembering our growing up years in Mansfield during the 1950s and 1960s? Maybe the episode with the twins crossed her mind.

My mind moved forward to Jurdine and John taking me to the train station the morning I left home to attend Southern University in Baton Rouge. She had by now been married for several years and was the mother of one girl and two boys.

It was difficult for me to leave. But I wanted to "make something of myself," so I was anxious to seize the opportunity. More than anything, though, I wanted to make a difference. I wanted to change the conditions my family and other folks were forced to endure just because they happened to be Black. But would I ever feel as warm and as cared for again as I did in that close-knit, nurturing Black community in Mansfield?

"You study hard, Brother," Jurdine said as we waited for the train that morning. "But I know you will do good. You have always been smart."

"I'll do my best," I responded.

She turned to her husband. "Baton Rouge is a long way, isn't it, John?"

John nodded his head.

"You be careful, Brother. And if anybody bothers you, just call me. And Big Sister will be in Baton Rouge in a flash."
She laughed.

I watched Jurdine wave furiously as the train pulled away. Was she thinking about that departure as we stared into each other's eyes in that hospital room?

Eight days had passed since I had been with Jurdine in the hospital. Her doctors felt she had gotten over the major hurdles and advised me that I could go back home, to New Jersey. "Everything should be all right," one of them said.

The night before my plane's departure, I stayed longer than usual with Jurdine. I told Jurdine that my wife and I still planned to have her and John visit us for the summer.

"You got to continue to improve, you know," I told her.

She smiled, nodded her head, and looked away.

I should have known then. Looking back, I believe she knew it would be the last time we would see each other. But I have always been an optimist.

Several days after I'd arrived back home, we got a call that Jurdine was in a coma again. Then, the following evening I got a call from her youngest daughter. "Brother," she said, trying to fight back the tears, "Mama's gone. She's gone, Brother."

I hung up the phone very deliberately and just stood, staring at the floor.

My wife held me as I sobbed. Then, slowly I gathered myself. "I have to tell the others . . . and we have to tell Ma'Dear and Daddy."

Over and over I asked myself why. Why Jurdine? Why now, at age 55?

We all made our way to Mansfield.

It had been a long time since I had been to my hometown. I wanted my children and my wife to see some of the places where we Hudson children played and learned. I wanted my family to meet some of the people who had helped to shape my life.

The day before the funeral, I took them to see my old high school. It was closed now. Today, all youngsters, Black and White, attend the same schools.

I took my family to see the old baseball field where I played the game I loved so much as a youngster. We went to Mary Street, where the house in which I had grown up had burned down long ago, and I pointed out all the short cuts we used to take on our way to school or to our grandmother's house, and the field where we played football. My family got a chance to meet some of those ladies who had been second mothers to all of us: Mrs. Ella Henderson, Mrs. Ella Lee, Mrs. Rebecca Hall. Mrs. Lee and Mrs. Hall, both in their 80s, could barely walk.

That night, I could not sleep. Images of Jurdine played in my mind the entire night.

The next day, at the country church where the funeral was held, so many people told me how Jurdine had helped them in their time of need. They recalled how she was never quick to judge them, no matter what the problem. One of my high school classmates told me how he would go to Jurdine's house for lunch during his senior year.

"I wouldn't have made it through had it not been for her," he said tearfully.

His parents were too poor to pay for his lunch and couldn't even provide him with a lunch to carry to school. "I didn't know you ate at her house," I said.

"I did," he replied, clutching his hat because he really didn't know what to do with his hands.

As we laid Jurdine's body to rest, I murmured through tears, "It just isn't right! Not right!"

"Don't say that, son," said my father, as he put a comforting hand on my shoulder. "It's tough, but we all have to do the same thing."

I whispered, "I love you!" to Jurdine again as the tears flowed.

Later, sitting alone, I thought about my oldest sister once more. I could see her as a teenager, teaching me how to dance. She was always such a great dancer. I could see her on her wedding day, walking down the steps in her white gown, as beautiful as an angel. I saw her in her kitchen, cooking all kinds of cakes and pies and other dishes. I saw her beaming as she held up a handful of toys she had purchased for her children.

I saw her face light up as she introduced me to a friend of hers. "This is the oldest of my brothers. He's a writer. Chile, he owns his own book publishing company. He helped people get the right to vote, too." Her face glowed with love and pride. "We look a lot alike, don't we?"

I did a lot of smiling as I thought back to those days. ∎

Smiley and Sylvia Fletcher's Family at Daily Prayer
Philadelphia, PA 1988
© Roland Freeman

Rock of Ages

by Tonya Bolden
photograph by Roland Freeman

*I was born into and raised up in a Black church, a very old-fashioned,
profoundly folk kind of church. But when I got grown and very educated
I decided to walk my own road. In time, I found that the worship of my
mind led only to a wasteland. So I did a turn-about from my walk-away
from God. And the Black Church.*

She plays Bach, and the tambourine.

Her name is Mother Zion Baptist All-Souls Sanctified Rock Creek
    A.M. E. Mount Mariah C. M. E. Marion Avenue A. M. E. Zion
    Church of the Good Shepard True Believers at the Cross
    Straight Street Congregational
    St. Mary's Lutheran
    St. Peter's R. C.
    St. Mark's Methodist
    St. Philip's Presbyterian
    Bethel Full-Gospel
    Shiloh.

She has done so much to make her people strong
    to keep so many alive in their bodies, in their souls.
    Multitudes she has mothered
    in times of dense distress.

When she was invisible . . .
    her roof nightsky,
    her flooring Godgrown pastures walled by woods . . .
    quiet streams did steal away to her
    preachments and soul-toned singing
    for the grit to go on, the might to keep the faith

and hold tight to Blessed Assurance that
Liberation was in holy order
with Nat Turner, Gabriel and Nancy Prosser,
Denmark, Harriet, Frederick
among her sons and daughters.

When she came to be seen–in timber, in brick, in stone–
    she remained a refuge of resistance
    where the 'buked and scorned assembled
    to be renewed in the spirit to be fortified in the mind
    to help themselves heal, stand up, stand tall.

Wasn't it she who raised in singles and change much money
    for raising schools, associations, old folks homes,
    for doing doing doing:
    when the Thompson family got burned out,
    when Brother Payne passed and his widow had no mite,
    when Sister Mayhew took sick,
    when badbutt Jasper was hungry?

When we were the not-alloweds
    and the go-to-the-back-door people,
    she was a warm place to be
    treasurer, trustee, M.C.
    Cradle, too, was she, for creative fire:
    where Aretha, Leontyne, Sam, Dinah, Della found voice,
    where Baldwin laid hands on rhythms he worked
    with words,
    where Martin learned to speak.

Most everywhere her pastors, elders, the business board,
    the deacons–men, with women
    piloting pageants, corralling committees,
    frying the chicken, crying with the sick,
    pulling Rev's coattail by withholding their Amens . . .
    taking girls and boys to Sunday School

to learn basic Bible stories and about the Lord and
to sit up straight and not fidget . . .
encouraging slackers to buck up and get dignity with
their mere presence in Sunday Best–
those marvelous hats, neat shoes, pressed dresses,
pocketbooks never without handkerchief
and peppermint balls . . .
gathering in prayer bands to war against
woes and wrongs.

She lives in cathedralettes, in city-brick and faux stained glass,
    in stubby storefronts, in clapboard A-frames
    in Philly, in 'Frisco, in N'Orleans, New York City, Kansas City,
    Kannapolis, Indianapolis, Baltimore, Boston, Austin, Laurel,
    Greenwood . . .

Arms ever-always open–
    through the neglect and disrespect, lack, attack
    the ashes–
    to embrace the children of her children's children
    and their child
    to be born. ■

Roots Go Deep

by Cheryl Willis Hudson

Recently, old photographs from Momma's attic have found their way out of dusty scrapbooks and into shiny frames and are proudly displayed in my living room. Words of wisdom in letters from my grandmother and faintly recalled incidents from my childhood have found their way into our story books for children.

When we were growing up, Daddy and Mom took time to remind my brothers and me of our strong family ties and proud heritage. I remember how Daddy sometimes recited poetry and old sayings to reinforce those connections.

"Surely our roots go deep," Momma was fond of saying during our trips to informal family reunions each summer in her hometown, Charlottesville, Virginia. Daddy would usually follow with, "Our vines have tender blossoms," referring to the innocence of the family's younger generation.

Momma's side of the family, the Watsons, were a loud, gregarious, and sociable bunch. "The Watson Clan" is how they referred to themselves, and clannish they were. They would entertain each other with stories of working in service, or in hotels or on the railroad. They were creative, too. They cooked and sewed, partied, played cards, laughed heartily, and were faithful and ever-ready when it came to getting together for one special occasion or another.

And there were lots of them. Great Grandma Watson had raised 13 children plus some. Dozens and dozens of cousins and aunts and uncles and friends of the family gathered every summer to celebrate Annie Scott Watson's birthday, to pay their respects to one who had lived for so long. And each year, as she drew closer and closer to her one hundredth year, the size of the family increased and so did the stories.

In the small town and in the family houses on 6 1/2 Street, formerly known as Watson's Bottom, there were lots of tales to tell. When the conversations started getting louder and louder, my brothers and I imagined that we were the "vines" and our ears the "blossoms" that weren't supposed to hear some of the juicier tidbits. But we ran in and out of screen doors, up and down the red clay hills, along the narrow streets and listened anyway.

The Willis family, on the other hand, whom we visited on our way back from Charlottesville, was much more reserved. They lived in the Church Hill section of Richmond, Virginia. Grandma Isaleen Spurlock Willis, my father's mother, had at the age of 82 purchased a home on North 22nd Street, and she lived there all by herself.

Momma often remarked on her mother-in-law's extremely neat and clean house and on her beautiful handwriting. As a child, I wondered why that was so important. After all, adults were *supposed* to know how to write and keep house, weren't they?

It was only much later that I realized and appreciated how rare it was for a person of Grandma Willis's age and race to be able to read and write so well with so little formal education. Her father, Henry Spurlock, was born a slave in 1812. In time he became a glazier and bought his freedom and some property, too.

When Grandma Willis bought her house on North 22nd, she still had a copy of the deed to her father's property on Marshall Street, sometimes call "I" Street—"sold to Henry Spurlock, freedman on July 16, 1868." He was 56 years old at the time.

Besides our nuclear family, the Willises consisted of Uncle Bill and Aunt Lil', Aunt Mary, Aunt AuVal, Uncle Alvin, and our cousins Jean and Alice. We heard no loud talking on our visits there. Hayes, Roderick, Orion, and myself had to sit very still in Grandma's parlor while the grown folks talked. And even though our visits were relatively short, it seemed an eternity before we were excused and allowed to rock (gently) back and forth on the wooden swing that hung from hooks on Grandma's front porch.

Grandma Willis had a sense of humor, but it was wry and dry. She inquired about our schoolwork, nodded her head and we watched her smile take a while to work its way up to the corners of her mouth.

I am warmed and encouraged by memories of those family visits and by snatches of stories from both my parents and their parents and their parents' parents. It does my heart good, too, that today our vines, our son and daughter, want to hear about the days when my husband and I were little and want to know whose side of the family they take after. At annual family reunions, they are amazed to see something of themselves in the new cousins they meet or in the pictures of the old ones who have passed on. Together, we are discovering more about our rich and living history. We know our roots go deep. ∎

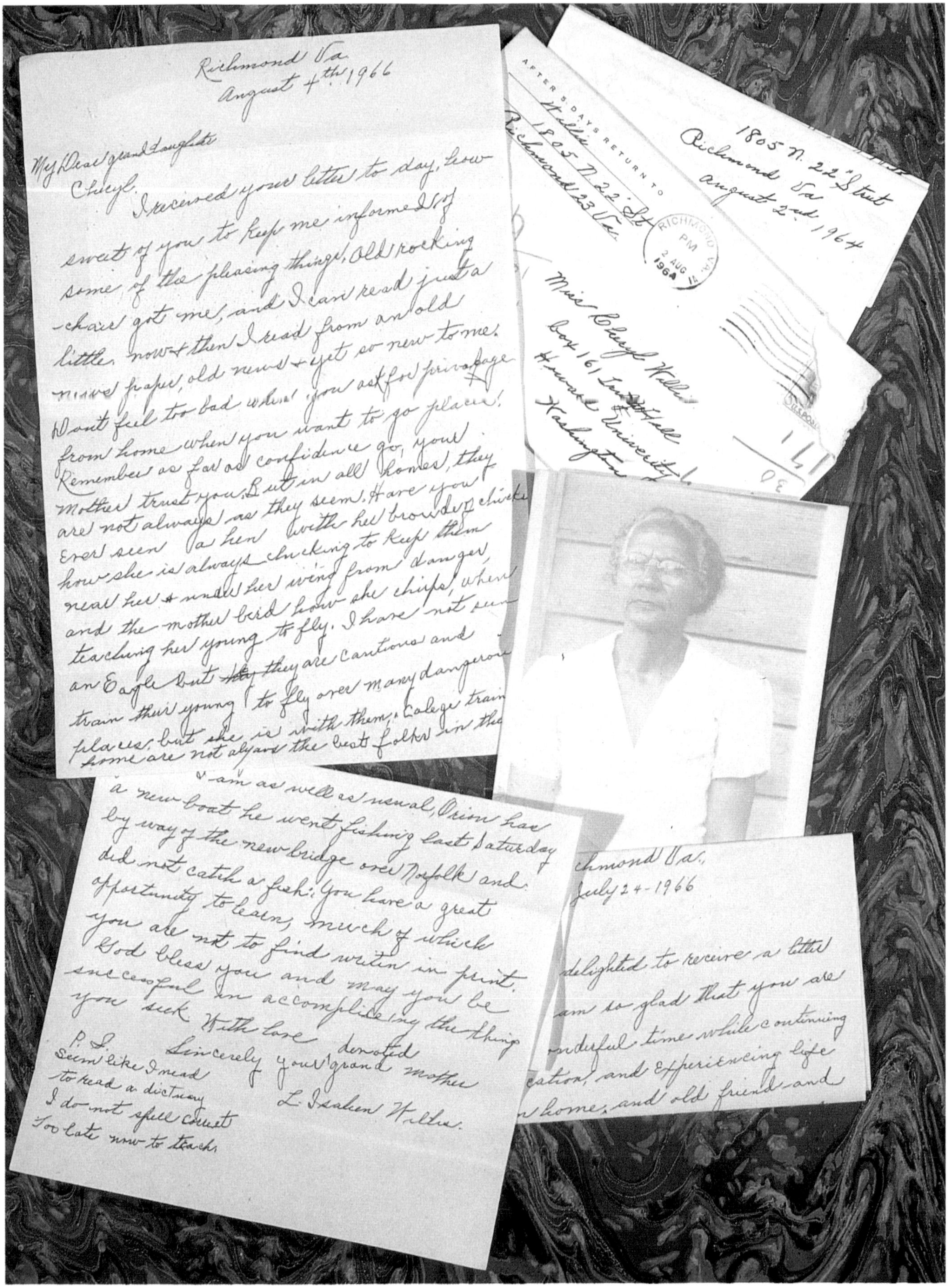

Richmond Va.
August 4th 1966

My Dear grand daughter
Cheryl, I received your letter to day, how
sweet of you to keep me informed I of
some of the pleasing things, Old rocking
chair got me, and I can read just a
little, now & then I read from an old
news paper, old news & yet so new to me.
Dont feel too bad when you ask for privalage
from home when you want to go places,
Remember as far as confidence go, your
Mother trust you. But in all homes, they
are not always as they seem. Have you
Ever seen a hen with her brood of chicks
how she is always clucking to keep them
near her & under her wing from danger,
and the mother bird how she chirps, when
teaching her young to fly. I have not seen
an Eagle but they they are cautious and
train their young to fly over many dangerous
places, but she is with them. Colege trained
home are not always the best folks in the

I am as well as usual, Orion has
a new boat he went fishing last Saturday
by way of the new bridge over Norfolk and
did not catch a fish. You have a great
opportunity to learn, much of which
you are not to find writen in print.
God bless you and may you be
suceessful in accomplishing the thing
you seek. With love
P.S. Sincerely your devoted grand mother
Seem like I read   L. Isaben Wolls
to read a dictnary
I do not spell corret
Too late now to teach.

1805 N. 22nd Stret
Richmond Va
August 2nd 1964

AFTER 5 DAYS RETURN TO
Wolls
1805 N 22 St
Richmond 23 Va.

Miss Cheryl Wolls
Box 161 Truthville
Howard University,
Washington

Richmond Va.
July 24 - 1966

delighted to receive a letter
I am so glad that you are
wonderful time while continuing
cation, and experiencing life
home, and old friend and

The Newman family's first home in Holt County, Nebraska, probably looked very much like this one belonging to the Shores family of Custer County.

Lydia M. Holmes
The Knockdown Wheeled Toy
No: 2,529,692   Patented November 14, 1950

Sam and Caroline Newman's daughter and son-in-law: Walter and Lydia Holm(e)s.

Nana

by *Glennette Tilley Turner*

As a child growing up in the Southeast, I was often transported to another time and place when my maternal grandmother, Nana, told me family stories. Especially the one about how toward the end of Reconstruction her parents, Sam and Caroline (Spurlark) Newman, and their children, Sam Jr. and Calpurnia, left Virginia in a covered wagon and headed West.

Their eventual destination was Nebraska, but they had to make an important stop along the way: my great-grandmother was expecting a baby. The plan was to reach her sister's home in Belvidere, Illinois, before the baby was due and deliver there. But the baby didn't wait for Belvidere. Great Grandma went into labor in Marengo, Illinois, about 12 miles from her sister's home. Making inquiries of the townspeople, my great-grandparents learned that a Black Civil War nurse by the name of Rachel Harris, lived in that town. They located Mrs. Harris, and she delivered the baby. Great Grandma Newman and her newborn, Aaron, wintered with her sister, and in the spring, they completed their westward journey on the train, which had just recently begun to go as far west as Nebraska.

Great Grandma and Grandpa Newman settled in Holt County, Neighly Township, to claim land under the Homestead Act that would become a

160-acre farm. Early on, the family lived in a sod house. It was warm in the winter, cool in the summer, and covered with wildflowers in the springtime. (It also had its disadvantages–like the time a skunk made its way into the sod house and "perfumed it.")

Building a permanent house was a slow process, for in Nebraska trees were few and far between. Once a year, Great Grandpa Newman would go "north," probably to Dakota, to get lumber. Eventually the family was able to move into a clapboard house, the kind with the planks arranged in an upright pattern that you see in old movies. This was preferable to the sod house, but it was not airtight. After a winter storm, the family would often awaken to find stripes across the beds where snow had blown in between the vertical cracks.

The scarcity of trees had an impact on farming as well. Trees made effective wind-breakers: without them to form barriers, dust storms could destroy a whole year's crops. Tree planting became a priority. In fact, Arbor Day was started in Nebraska.

And so, while Great Grandpa Newman and the children planted crops and trees, Great Grandma Newman spun wool for socks, gloves, and caps, and made other clothing from flax or store-bought cotton. And she cooked for the family and the hired men, ironed, cleaned, cared for the vegetable garden, and bore children–she was also a midwife.

About two years after Great Grandma Newman reached Nebraska with Aaron, a daughter, Martha Rebecca, was born. Her birth was followed at two-year intervals by the births of another boy, Jim, and a girl, Mary Lydia, who grew up to be my Nana– who told me rich family stories.

The Newman's pioneering spirit didn't bypass my grandmother's generation. Two brothers became cowboys. Over the years one sister cared for 100 foster children. Another sister became a movie actress. My grandmother became an inventor.

Nana had an uncanny ability to see new uses for everyday things. When she was older she and her youngest daughter came to live with my parents–her oldest daughter, Phyllis, and son-in-law, John. While caring for my brother John Jr. and me, Nana would make pull-toys for us out of items such as large wooden spools and evaporated milk cans. She made a chewing gum holder from a walnut shell and fashioned a planter from a coconut shell. She used to cut plywood into toys and planters with a hand-held coping saw.

One Christmas, my parents gave her what proved to be *the* perfect gift: an electric jigsaw. Nana loved it. Each night, she would hurriedly finish the dishes and spend hours creating. The Christmas display in which she had the Three Wise Men and their camels move on a conveyor belt past a scene of Bethlehem was so intriguing to me.

As a child, I never realized how remarkable my grandmother was. Imagine my great joy when I found out that she had even created a patent-worthy toy: "The Knockdown Wheeled Toy." Her patent number 2,529,692 was granted on November 14, 1950. Sadly, Nana never knew her patent was issued: she died before it was granted. But eventually her name was added to the long list of once unknown African-American inventors, and, of course, Nana's own story became one of my favorites. ∎

Kazumi's Shelf

by Toyomi Igus

photograph by Roland Charles

My daughter, Kazumi, sprawls her five-foot eight-inch frame in front of the television set and laughs at the antics of some adolescent comic actor. I watch her and marvel at the young woman emerging. At 12, she is already showing signs that she will become all that I hope she will be.

As is usual when my maternal emotions engulf me, my thoughts turn to Kazumi's grandmother: my mother, Kazumi Tamori. I look for signs in my daughter's face and form that would remind me of my mother. At first glance, the two Kazumis do not look anything alike: my daughter (Zumi, as we call her) has the mahogany-colored skin of her father, the height and lean physique inherited from both her parents. She is a tall, becoming, graceful girl in a baby tee, baggy-but-not-too-baggy jeans, Fila sneakers, and braids that won't sweat out during her biweekly basketball practices.

But then you notice the epicanthic fold of the eyes–ah, yes, there are the genes. The curve of the cheek–that's Mom, the young Kazumi Tamori. The overwhelming kindness, the quiet strength, the inner resolve–definitely Mom.

Kazumi Tamori, my mother, was Japanese, born on the island of Honshu, in the Gifu province, I am told, in 1926. For years she made us all believe she was born in 1930, the same year as my father, Will Gibson, the MP she became enamored with post-World War II. Almost 10 years after my mother's death, I named my daughter after her as she had named me–Toyomi–after her own mother. As I miss her, I guess she missed her mom–the grandmother I never knew just as my daughter never knew hers.

Doesn't seem to matter, though. The knowing comes from me–through me and my descriptions of my mother, my remembrances, the lessons she taught me, consciously or not, that I now pass on to my girl child, consciously or not.

And, amazingly, magically, my daughter Zumi responds. There is a connection between the young Kazumi and the old. It has taken physical shape on a special shelf in my daughter's room. On this shelf, in this little cubicle, is all of the material evidence I had of Kazumi Tamori to share with her. Trinkets, clothing, knick-knacks that survived my own turbulent journey to Los Angeles and motherhood to be discovered, dusted off, and placed with reverence on Kazumi's shelf.

Never mind that this shelf would remind my mother of a Shinto Buddhist altar in tribute to our ancestors. Never mind that my daughter is oblivious to that fact. To Zumi, her grandmother is her own personal guardian angel, so Zumi's shelf is of her own design, of her own imagining. And it upholds the beginnings of my preteen daughter's understanding of her heritage and her identity.

I will share with you a glimpse into Kazumi's shelf:

In the center is a jewelry box. This box was my mother's gift to me after a trip to Japan to visit her father. I'm not exactly sure (I have to check with Dad about this), but that trip could have been Mom's only return to her homeland after she emigrated to America to join the young African-American soldier-turned-law student and his family in the corn fields of Iowa. I remember very clearly when my diminutive mother—barely five feet in her *zoris*—went on this trip because Mom *never* went away. In typical Japanese tradition, my mother was always with her children.

I have since seen replicas of this jewelry box in the Japantown souvenir shops of New York and Los Angeles. It is made of plastic with a faux wood grain. It stands on four peg legs and has two doors that open to reveal three little drawers on the left (for holding your jewelry) and a painting of

roses on the right. It is a musical box, but oddly (or not so oddly if you understand the Japanese fascination with the Western world), it plays "The Anniversary Song," a Western classical tune, when the doors are opened. As I write this, it dawns on me that this gift to me may have spawned my own tradition of giving my children music boxes.

I cherished this box as much as my daughter now does. Not only had my mother chosen it for me, but it had actually come from *Nihon*, that foreign, far-away place where I had family, roots, history.

The bottom drawer of the jewelry box holds a large fake-ruby ring that was my mother's. Almost every other piece of my mother's jewelry was either given away or lost over the years—yet this ring survived. Zumi first spied it in a box of my costume jewelry we rummaged through during her four-year-old fairy-princess stage. It was adjustable, so could fit perfectly on her toddler finger.

I remember my mother admiring this ring in a catalog and actually ordering it. It struck me then—as it does now—as strange. Mom was never a gaudy-jewelry-wearing kind of woman. She was classic Audrey Hepburn, Lena Horne, or Grace Kelly. Basic black and pearls. Evoke a strong yet quiet feminine presence, but never draw attention to yourself—this was her unspoken lesson to me.

Draped gracefully in front of the jewelry box on Kazumi's shelf are two articles of clothing that speak volumes about who my mother was. The first to catch your eye is a frayed golden Lurex blouse, cropped, cap-sleeved, with pearl buttons—simple yet once very elegant. To be worn with a black velvet skirt while sipping martinis. To Zumi, it would be very retro and she would probably wear it frequently during her mall cruises if it weren't for the fact that the blouse is so small.

It hits me like a heart attack. Here it is. Here *she* is. One tattered blouse–some unreal size 2–and my mother's shape, form, presence becomes embodied. How could Kazumi Tamori have been so small? The memories are so big.

Next to the blouse, a crocheted apron. I'm not sure that Kazumi actually crocheted this apron herself. She very well could have–and I prefer to think that she did. She was an accomplished seamstress and made all of the clothes I remember best as a young girl. She taught me to sew, knit, and crochet–skills I now feel obligated to pass on to Zumi, skills that have become lost to most contemporary American girls.

But the apron recalls much more to me than my mother's creative talents. It represents the antithesis of what the Lurex blouse symbolizes. It is Mom–the homemaker who took great pleasure in building her home with style. Mom–the nurturer who would stay up all hours of the night with me, bringing me tea as I crammed for a Latin exam. Mom–fulfilling her role as mother, as she understood it to be, during a time when the role of mother–indeed, the role of *woman*–was being redefined all around her, in turmoil and flux.

Look to the left on the shelf and you will see an English bone-china cup and saucer. A bit chipped here and there, but intact. It does not surprise me that Zumi found the cup and wheedled its history from me. Like her grandmother, Zumi is a collector of pretty things.

This cup and saucer set was only one of many that my mother collected and stored in the china cabinet in our old rambling Buffalo, New York, home and the last of the many china and crystal knickknacks that lived in that cabinet. The story of its survival is long, elaborate, and sad. Suffice it to say that it found its way to Zumi's shelf after having been found and lost and found and lost by my brother, my sisters, and me after my mother died suddenly in 1975.

Many things were lost when Mom died. I mean that figuratively and literally–like the foot-high Japanese doll: a woman in traditional Japanese dress, who was housed, like all such handmade dolls, inside a glass box on my mother's sideboard. It is lost. But a smaller replica lives on Kazumi's shelf–a contribution to my daughter from her Grandpa.

And tucked beside the doll, the image of the guardian angel–a photograph of a young Kazumi Tamori in all of her ethereal beauty. And there I can see the fold of the eyes, the curve of the cheek, the inner resolve that fortified the young Japanese woman and prepared her for her journey to the land of the conqueror, the enemy, the land of her future, her legacy . . .

Which live on in the five-foot eight-inch frame of my beautiful African-American daughter. ■

Faith Ringgold
The Bitter Nest Part 2: The Harlem Renaissance Party, 1988
Acrylic on canvas; printed, tie-dyed, and pieced fabric
94 x 82 inches
artist's collection

Momma's Kitchen Table

by *Eleanora E. Tate*
story-quilt by *Faith Ringgold*

My grandmother, whom I called Momma, and her kitchen table have been part of my life as far back as I can remember, which is back to the early 1950s, in the tiny Mississippi River town of Canton, Missouri. At the kitchen table I ate the hated shredded wheat as well as oatmeal and white rice, which I loved. If I were eating breakfast on a winter's Monday morning, I could watch steam from boiling navy beans and hamhocks send streaks of water down the window panes while Momma piled one end of the table with blue jeans, shirts, skirts, and underwear that she had washed and pulled from the wringer of her Maytag. Under the red and white checkered oilcloth tablecloth, the table had been painted white. Under my care, I painted it bright yellow, then later stripped it down to its original brown wood identified with a metal nameplate of the manufacturer: Sellers of Elwood, Indiana.

One of the sayings I learned from Momma at the table was, "A hard head makes a soft behind," though she sometimes didn't say "behind." For years I didn't understand what that saying meant, but I can remember a time when she applied it to something I'd done. I was probably four or five years old and at Green's ice cream parlor, where my favorites–chocolate chip ice cream and lime and orange sherbet– waited for me in their bins. Didn't matter that it was winter. I loved my ice cream. The way that I remember it is that I wanted to sit on the barstool, but in my snowsuit I was too fat to make the climb. Momma warned me not to do it, but I tried anyway. Of course, I hit the floor and the barstool hit me. As she set me and the stool back on our legs, she told me, "A hard head makes a soft . . . behind." I've fallen off many a barstool since that time, and in more ways than one, but by now I've learned to at least think twice before risking my behind on just anything.

Once or twice a month on a Saturday afternoon Momma's kitchen table became our beauty parlor and held the weapons of woman's beauty–the infamous hair rep (or Vaseline in a pinch), the wide-tooth comb perched in her pearl-handled hair brush, and the precious hot comb and curling iron. I sat by the gas stove in a kitchen chair with a towel wrapped around my shoulders, with one side of my head still covered by my short kinky hair (always under attack by do-gooder relatives determined to make it grow), the other side newly and safely made oily smooth from the smoking hot comb.

Having captured me at the kitchen table this way, Momma would often tell me about her own childhood adventures. The one I remember most vividly was the time she rode a friend's sled down a hill, tore her underpants to pieces, and ran into a tree at the bottom. She also liked to warn me of what happened to kids who didn't behave according to the wisdom of their grand parents. These ruffians usually ended up suffering the most horrible consequences. Some tumbled into wells because they wouldn't stay put. Some were kidnapped and never heard from again.

It was at the kitchen table during hair-pressing time that I learned to respect people's age. The nearby tabletop radio usually would be tuned to a St. Louis station playing Ray Charles, Clyde McPhatter,

and LaVern Baker. If her spirits were up, Momma would hum as she pressed my little hair or sometimes, to my delight, tell me about how men used to love her big legs, and even do a little dance step.

Well, one time I forgot that I was still a child and teased her by saying, "You're too old to dance."

Instantly, the humming and dancing stopped, and I got this feeling of impending doom. Momma plucked me HARD on the back of my head with her middle finger. She would NEVER get too old to dance, or at least to pat her foot, she said, and it wasn't NOBODY'S business but her own.

Like many families, ours survived because, in the wake of my mother's divorce, my grandmother pitched in with the raising of my older sister, brother, and me. My mother moved to Des Moines, Iowa, where jobs for Black women were easier to get at that time. Our grandmother, at the age of 45 or so, took on the task of raising three children. As my siblings grew to adulthood, first my sister, then my brother joined my mother in Des Moines.

When I turned 13 in 1961, I followed, too, and left Momma and her kitchen table behind–but not alone. I left instructions with one of Momma's lady friends to give Momma a puppy from the litter that her dog was about to have. She did, and Momma became the owner of a puppy she named Randy. More important, though, Momma got married to a dapper, kindly, gold rim eye-glassed Baptist deacon from a nearby town.

Meanwhile, I survived my turbulent teens, though I had to learn several times in the process that a hard head makes a soft behind. I became a single mother, determined though to work and make my own way, without welfare, and even go to college and become a journalist.

In 1965, my grandmother's husband passed away. By 1970, everybody, including my grandmother, was living in Des Moines. Momma's kitchen table came, too, and shortly thereafter became mine.

I don't recall any fanfare when the table changed hands. It was simply a matter of my needing a kitchen table for my latest apartment, and Momma, in her own apartment with a brand new Formica and metal table, gave the old one to me.

For a number of reasons–one of which was that I was the youngest–I'd always felt that I was on the fringe of so many family matters, but Momma and I were buddies and in many ways she was a protective buffer for me. She and I also confided in each other, no matter how many miles we were apart.

In 1976 Momma's kitchen table and I hit the road. This time we–along with my husband, Zack, my daughter, and our dog– headed for Tennessee. In 1978 we moved to the beer-guzzling, green-pants-and-yellow-golf-shirt-wearing, biker-beach-bikini, so-called family resort of Myrtle

Beach, where Zack was stationed at the U.S. Air Force Base.

Myrtle Beach in the late 1970s was newly desegregated. Located in a county that had been isolated geographically from the rest of the state and world by swamps, rivers, and the Atlantic Ocean, the Horry County African-American and White populations lived in a time warp that still maintained a "de boss man" and "de boss lady" atmosphere. In a state whose heritage was thick with slave revolts (the Stono Rebellion, for one) noted African Americans (Denmark Vesey, Benjamin Mays, Mary McLeod Bethune, and dozens of others), it was sad to see so much subservience within the Black community.

Professional jobs for African Americans were limited, and I was turned down at least three times by White newspapers, despite my having a journalism degree and experience as a reporter for many years with the *Des Moines Register* and *Tribune* newspapers. I was rejected over more than 30 times from even mundane sales jobs at places like K-Mart. About the only thing left for me to do was to write, and even that was difficult.

But it was at Momma's kitchen table that I completed what became my first published book for children, *Just an Overnight Guest*, about what happens when a Black family takes in a neglected child.

After my book was published, I continued to have difficulty finding a job, so I decided to start selling news stories to African-American newspapers around South

Carolina through our Positive Images News Service.

Things began to look up when J. John French, Sr., publisher of the *Charleston Chronicle*, became a wonderful friend and supporter of our tiny news service. (He told me that he'd begun his newspaper on his kitchen table.) Our business quickly spread throughout the county–and the kitchen table began a new career as a layout and design unit. Zack's photos of choirs, children at play, cemetery scenes, public officials, and "first Black Named . . ." were laid out to dry on its surface. Program books pages commissioned by sororities, churches, housing agencies, and civic and social organizations took shape on the top of Momma's kitchen table, too. In place of meat loaf, mashed potatoes, and pinto beans sat the tools of the table's new trade– bottles of white-out, stacks of paper, type- writer ribbons, clip art books, dummy sheets, galley proofs, a waxing machine, a paper cutter.

Stories piled up–about Atlantic Beach, South Carolina, the all-Black beachfront town, about the county's heroic and hypo- critical civil rights endeavors, about Ku Klux Klan marches through Myrtle Beach's oceanside boulevards, about the old Black cemetery's pioneers, and finally, in 1991, an avalanche of information and stories about a national festival of Black storytelling that we brought, with the help of friends, to the county. The kitchen table became as valuable a piece of equipment as my computers and Zack's cameras.

Though Momma had always been an adventurer, she had never traveled far from home. It was clearly a great adventure when, in her late 70s, she boarded an airplane for the first time in her life and, with my mother, flew from Iowa to South Carolina to visit us for several wonderful days. The highlight of the visit was when everyone in robes and pajamas gathered around the kitchen table for a "rise 'n' fly" checkers tournament. Momma, always one who loved this game, sometimes conve- niently changed the rules depending on whether she was winning or losing. But I didn't mind. It was just glorious to see her enjoyment, and to feel my own.

And in the last few years of her life, our telephones and our inner bond kept us in touch. Once when I was at home and she was in a senior citizens', home in Des Moines, I felt an especially urgent need to call her, so I did. Imagine my surprise when she told me that only a short time earlier she'd fallen and slightly injured her wrist. "But I'm okay now, and I sure am glad to hear your voice. Nobody else but the nurse and you even knows yet."

I was fortunate to have been able to visit her in 1983, three weeks before she died. In those last painful days we had lain with our heads together on her pillow in the hospital room and talked and talked. She asked me if she could come live with me in South Carolina, knowing though, that such a move wasn't possible, I couldn't have taken care of her, and she wouldn't have been able to leave, anyway. But we were able to talk about it, and take solace in the fact that I wanted her.

Momma died May 12, 1983, at the age of 81, and was buried beside her last husband in Canton's cemetery on the Mississippi River bluffs.

At the time she died, Zack and I had just started a project to produce a cookbook for a Myrtle Beach landmark "soulfood" restaurant called "Mrs. Frances' Kitchen," operated by Mrs. Frances Bowen; her husband, Prince; and son, Prince, Jr. Within days of Momma's death, Mrs. Bowen died, too. Completing the cookbook became even more important to her son, who had commissioned the project, and to me: it helped us both channel our anguish into something positive.

I was also trying to write another book, this time about South Carolina. One day, sitting at the kitchen table and looking at photos I'd taken Memorial Day at an old Black cemetery left to grow to weeds, and thinking of Momma so recently deceased, something began to form in my mind. I drove over to the cemetery and walked among the graves, thinking about the lost history of so many of Myrtle Beach's African-American pioneers. Mourning for my grandmother, thinking of my surroundings, *The Secret of Gumbo Grove* came to life.

Momma's kitchen table has been a storyteller of sorts, for sitting around it so often makes me think back on my childhood and the loving, short, hard-working, brown-skinned woman who fed me cherry cobbler there and who, as she pressed my hair, talked to me there, and did her best to raise me right. ∎

Sugar

by Joyce Carol Thomas
photograph by John Pinderhughes

Mama says,
"To feed you when you
were a baby
I mashed wild berries
Sweet as the taste of your dimples
When I kissed them"

And then she coos,
"Give me some sugar"
And I smother her cheeks with kisses

My mouth remembers those berries
I taste them still
The tangy flavors
The luscious colors

I try hard to stay as sweet
As berries in July
But sometimes my mood is so sour
It puckers my lips

And Mama says,
"I like you just as you are
Sour or sweet"

And she gives me that Mama smile
Patient as summer
Waiting for berries to ripen

Ornaments

by *Patricia C. and Fredrick McKissack, Jr.*

illustration by Higgins Bond

My grandmother Melinda was the youngest of the three Maywood girls who grew up in the big white Victorian house at #7 Rusher Street in Thomasville, Tennessee. The house was built by Avery Maywood, in 1872 on property he had purchased after the Civil War. My earliest memory of the house on Rusher Street is Christmas 1959. It was the first of many Christmases I would spend at the old homeplace and the first time I saw three treasured ornaments and heard their stories.

My great aunts Amanda and Johnetta were widowed by 1959 and had come home to share the old house with Grandmother Melinda. They couldn't wait to introduce me to all my relatives whose unsmiling faces stared down at me from the parlor mantel. As we trimmed the Christmas tree, Grandmother and her sisters brought those stony images to life through a never-ending tapestry of stories.

When Grandmother found the first of the three ornaments, she carefully untied the pink ribbon and unwrapped the yellowed tissue paper. We all watched quietly as she removed a tiny crocheted angel ornament.

"It's very old," I said softly.

"Yes. My grandmother made it for me back in 1905," she said.

Melinda's Angel
Melinda didn't know what to think! Grandpa Maywood had been acting strangely all morning. She had followed him up the stairs and down again–in one room and out the other. He seemed to be searching for something. But he wouldn't say what.

She watched with wide, wondering eyes as Grandpa climbed up the steep attic steps to that dark shadowy place where scary thoughts lived. She remembered the time the attic door had stuck shut behind her, and she shivered with fear. She couldn't follow Grandpa there.

Melinda started to put her thumb in her mouth, but she put her hand behind her back instead and clutched

Jessie, the little scarf doll she carried all the time. "Grandpa?" Melinda called up the steps. "Are you all right?"

Of course he wasn't all right, Melinda decided. She hoped he'd be better by evening. They were going to decorate their Christmas tree.

Thump! Thump! Melinda could hear her grandfather dragging heavy boxes and pushing old furniture around. What was he looking for?

"Grandpa!" Melinda called out again. "What are you doing?"

The noises stopped suddenly. Silence. Melinda listened to the quiet. "Do you think Grandpa's heart attacked him like Grandma's did?" she asked Jessie.

What if Grandpa was sick? What if he needed her? Melinda had to go up the stairs to the attic to see. Tucking Jessie close to her heart, she slowly tiptoed up the steps, hoping that by being very quiet she wouldn't disturb the scary things that waited in the dark.

She peeked inside the attic room. A circle of light filtered through the small, round window. Grandpa was kneeling beside the old trunk, looking at things, old things.

"Grandpa," Melinda whispered. "I know how to get help if you need it."

Grandpa looked up, smiling. "Come," he said, beckoning for her to join him.

Fear locked Melinda's legs. "I'm scared," she said, wanting desperately to suck her thumb. "So is Jessie."

"I understand," said Grandpa. "I really do understand."

Then, with slow careful hands, he unfolded a package wrapped in crinkly tissue paper and tied with a pink bow. Inside was a beautiful hand-crocheted angel. "I finally remembered where your Grandma put this. She crocheted this angel for you. It was the last thing she made." He held up the angel in the circle of light.

Melinda took one small step into the dreaded room. At the same time, Grandpa stretched out his arms to receive her. She didn't feel alone or frightened anymore. She was surrounded by love. And that night they put Melinda's special angel on their tree.

■ ■ ■

Next, Grandmother Melinda showed me an ornament that needed repair. "Get the glue," she said. "Every year I have to touch it up here and there."

As she worked on it, she told me a wonderful story about my father, Ross. I never tired of hearing about how Daddy ate too many green apples, went skinny-dipping in the creek in the winter, and got a spanking for sassing Mrs. Russell, his third grade teacher. But this story was extra special.

Ross's Angel

When Grandmother Melinda was 18 years old, she married Daniel Ripley and the couple moved to Chicago. Ross Ripley, my father, was the youngest of their three children. His sister, Grace, was the oldest, and his brother, Thomas, was next.

The November Ross turned seven, Franklin Delano Roosevelt was elected president of the United States, and his daddy died. Times were hard, but Melinda knew they would be harder if she stayed in Chicago. Widowed and poor, she packed up her family and moved back to Thomasville, Tennessee. Grandmother Melinda's folks were still living then, and they welcomed their daughter and three grandchildren into the ancestral home.

By the following year, Melinda had met and married her second husband, Charles Bevels. He was a robust man with large hands and broad shoulders. He had a voice as large as his body, and when he laughed the chandelier tingled in the dining room. Everybody called him Big Dad; everybody was charmed by his warmth and generosity. All except Ross.

"He's not my daddy," Ross said defiantly. "And he'll never be my daddy."

Nobody knew how much Ross was hurting inside. He missed his father, but he was unable to express his feelings. Instead, he chose not to talk much, because he had developed a stutter. Adding to his problems, Ross was clumsy and slow to smile. Beside his brother and sister, who had sunny dispositions, he became a gray child who would just blend into the scenery. That's where he stayed, thinking nobody really cared.

Big Dad was fortunate enough to find work at the coal company in Nashville during the week. And that suited Ross just fine. But Big Dad came home on the weekends, covered in coal dust and hungry for Melinda's good cooking and attention. It wasn't until after Big Dad had taken a hot bath in a large tin tub and put on clean clothes that he'd greet everybody with huge hugs.

"Come to Big Dad," he always said, holding out big bear arms. Grace and Thomas bounded toward him, but Ross held back, clinging to Melinda's leg for security.

"What's wrong, Ross? Go on," she coaxed. But he wouldn't respond.

The weekend before Christmas, Big Dad came home dragging a freshly cut fir from Mr. Millerstone's woods. After his ritual bath, Big Dad brought in the stately tree and set it up in the large parlor where Maywood holiday trees had been standing for years. As usual at that time of the year, the house was noisy and full of wonderful smells. Mama Maywood and Melinda had been cooking Tennessee country ham, sweet potato casserole, oatmeal cookies, apple and pecan pies—and there was plenty of eggnog.

After dinner, the family sang songs and told a round of stories. Grace sat in Big Dad's lap, and Thomas was draped across the arm of his chair. There was no room for Ross, so he sat on the floor by the fireplace. He wondered how Grace and Thomas could be so happy with the new father-man. Somehow it all seemed disloyal and unfair to his real father. They've forgotten about him, Ross thought sadly.

Suddenly, Big Dad left the room. When he returned, he gave Melinda a small box. "I want you to open this now, even though it's not Christmas yet." His eyes were filled with expectation.

Inside was a beautiful glass angel ornament. "I thought it would look great on our first tree," Big Dad said smiling. Melinda responded with all kinds of *ooh*s and *aah*s. Ross looked away in disgust. "How can she get all excited about a dime store ditty?" he wondered sullenly, as his mother passed the little angel around for everyone to see.

When the angel reached Ross, it slipped from his hands and fell on the marble hearth, breaking into many pieces. "I-I-I-I'm s-s-sorry," he said, batting tears away. "H-h-honest. I didn't m-m-mean to drop it!"

Ross felt Big Dad's eyes on him. He felt small and frightened. But if he had looked more closely, he would have noticed that Big Dad's eyes showed no anger, just concern.

"He did it on purpose," Grace said, pointing an accusing finger.

"N-n-no, I didn't," Ross cried. "I wish Daddy w-w-would come back and w-w-we could be like we w-w-were." Now, he had said it. Said what he had wanted to say for a long time. But now that the words were set loose, he felt more troubled than relief. Confused and frustrated, Ross ran to his room.

A few minutes later, someone knocked on his bedroom door. "Go away!" he cried. But the door opened and in walked Big Dad.

"Okay," he said in his no-nonsense voice. "Up off that bed. There's work to do." He spread out the shattered glass angel on Ross's desk, and set down a bottle of glue. "We have to put this ornament back together for your mother or we'll both be outside sleeping in the doghouse."

For the rest of the evening, Ross and Big Dad worked on the angel. Big Dad's fingers were awkward and he fumbled. Ross took control. "No, like this," he said, managing the glue masterfully.

While they worked, they talked about lots of things, about loss, about being afraid, and about loving and caring.

"I miss my daddy so much," Ross said without stuttering.

Big Dad put his arm on Ross's shoulder. "I know you do, son."

Then putting the last piece of glass in place, Big Dad said, "this broken angel reminds me of how we can be sometimes—all busted, broken up, and chipped. But love is the glue that can help put us back together again."

"I get so scared and feel so alone."

"Son, I know about that, too. Tell you what . . . I can't take the place of your father. But may I offer myself as a loving stepfather?"

"I'd guess so—Big Dad."

After that Ross didn't feel alone or frightened anymore. He stopped stuttering, and grew into a happy, active boy.

Together, Big Dad and Ross had taken the repaired angel downstairs and put it on the tree.

Grandmother Melinda's eyes sparkled as she described how the lights glittered through the cracks making the little glass angel sparkle like crystal.

■ ■ ■

The last ornament Grandmother Melinda showed me was a little hand-carved wooden angel that had belonged to my late aunt Grace. "My brother Armstrong Maywood gave this to my baby back in thirty seven," she said.

"Where did it come from?" I asked, examining it under the light.

Grace's Angel
Uncle Armstrong taught history at a local college. During the Depression, he was hired by the government to gather stories from former slaves.

"Get dressed," Uncle Armstrong told Grace early one morning. "You might enjoy visiting my office."

His office always felt much smaller than it was because of the stacks of papers that lined the walls. Every corner was occupied by books, papers, and folders.

Even though the campus was closed during the holidays, Uncle Armstrong couldn't stay away from his work more than a few days. "He would have dried up and blown away," Grandmother Melinda liked to joke.

While he looked through his mail, Grace studied the books on his shelf. There was the autobiography of Frederick Douglass, the great abolitionist. The words were too hard for her to read, but Uncle Armstrong had read a piece to her about Douglass from *The Crisis*, published by the NAACP. She remembered the young slave's flight to freedom and wondered why some people were so cruel and filled with hate.

Uncle Armstrong decided to answer a few letters. Grace didn't mind. Her curious eyes moved around the office, taking in decades of her uncle's work. That's when she saw the small wooden angel, half-hidden by the appointment calendar and ink bottle. It was polished and gracefully carved. She'd never seen anything like it. Where had it come from?

"So you discovered it," Uncle Armstrong said, looking up from his work and pushing back in his chair. "It is an unusual piece. It was given to me by Mrs. Henrietta Grimes, a former slave on the Seven Oaks Plantation in Dexter County, Mississippi, whom I had the honor of interviewing."

"Did she carve it herself?"

"No. She said a man she called Daddy James did it. He was like a grandfather to her. Seems he gave this angel to her during the Big Times."

"Is that what the slaves called Christmas?"

"Yes, because it was the one time of the year they had enough to eat and enough time to eat it. It was also a good time to escape. Henrietta Grimes was eight when she and about five others ran away with the help of the conductors on the Underground Railroad. Ran away Christmas Day 1858. She told me she held on to this little angel every step of the way."

Grace studied the angel with excited fingers, letting the smooth wood tell her its own story.

"Just think," said Grace, "this little angel helped keep Henrietta Grimes from being scared during the dangerous journey to freedom. Whatever made her give it away?"

"The same reason I'm going to part with it. To keep the story alive. Mrs. Henrietta Grimes told me to tell the story. I have. Now I'm giving you the carving. Make sure you tell the story."

"I will," said Grace. And she did.

Every Christmas until her death, Grace put the carved angel ornament on the Christmas tree and told the story of how Henrietta Grimes escaped to freedom on Christmas Day 1858.

And every Christmas we tell the story, as we hang on our tree Grace's angel.

And Ross's angel.

And Melinda's angel, too.

You see, today I own the house on Rusher Street, and that makes me the volunteer custodian of the family treasures–and their stories. ■

Louisa Pilgrim

by George Ford

This is my happiest memory of the five child-hood years that my sister, Marguerita, and I spent living with our wonderfully gifted Grandma Lou–drawing and reading together on the steps of our little house in St. Michael's Parish, Barbados, W.I.–just up the road from The Turnin'.

"Fetching" Out of the Past

an interview with Virginia Hamilton

Mother was always telling me to go take a look at something. I came to understand that she meant for me to see things for myself. She was the most objective woman I've ever known, and she would never tell me what to think. She is perhaps the best reason I have for my seeing everything in my own individual way. She always said, "I trust you to do what is right, Virginia." First, I had to find out what "right" was!

What was your childhood like?

My childhood was wonderful. I grew up on a farm. I was the youngest of five children and exempt from most of the work. I remember summers, running free and playing with my cousins. We made up all sorts of games. Stilting was a big thing. We made our own stilts and stilted everywhere. Only recently have I learned that stilting goes back to Africa, is part of the heritage. In my book, *Willie Bea and the Time the Martians Landed*, there is a good amount of stilting. That's me, up there on the cover, stilting in the moonlight!

You are a wordsmith who works with images and ideas. Yet, many of your characters work with their hands. Do you have a special place in your heart for "regular" people–people of the land?

Ah, I come from the land. All of my mother's brothers owned farms contiguous with our farm. All of the womenfolk, including my mother, worked in the home, in the gardens, and used their hands. Mother had small, delicate hands. But the others had the thick hands of farm women. Yes, they were regular, wonderful farm people. I could roam all day–run in and out of houses for drinks of water, or cookies, or berries, and never leave relatives' property.

You tackle controversial issues in your books. Is this by design? Or is it impossible to write about Black experiences in America without dealing with controversy?

I think if you live in America and you are African American and a writer, you will naturally write about what you know. And I know all aspects of African-American life here. I have experienced practically every situation the majority of Blacks confront at one time or another, plus those situations in which I am "invisible". . . more or less. Lots of times, other ethnic groups don't recognize me as African American–because I take after my father, who was of rather light complexion. He and my mother are no longer living. My brothers and sisters and I range in color from deep brown to quite light. My mother was very brown.

I married outside of my race and have two biracial adult children. We say that my husband Arnold's people came out of Africa, as well–"*When Israel Was in Egypt Land,*" as the spiritual says. Arnold and I have been married for going on thirty-six years. "It ain't been easy," but it is never boring. I learned my egalitarian philosophy from both my father and mother, as did my husband from his parents. We really grew up believing that all people were of equal worth. We've passed that belief along to our children. Our children consider themselves biracial and not White, nor Black. They have the right, although people seeing them will consider them in one way or another and other ways. I believe they've come to terms with their combined heritage–they loved my mama to death, my whole Perry/Hamilton family, and they care about Arnold's mom, Grandma Rita, down in Florida and other Adoff relatives. They are like a new ethnic group, of which there are many people now.

I don't really set out to tackle controversial issues in my books. I just happened to have lived them, like Buhlaire, in *Plain City*, pale yellow and different. Like Zeely, in *Zeely*, six-feet tall and deeply dark, like a pole of Ceylon ebony. Like Arilla, in *Arilla Sun Down*, half Black, half Indian. There are Black Indians, living albeit uncomfortably, on reservations in this country. So many Blacks claim Amerindian heritage, as did my family. All that experience goes into my creations.

We've all had difficulties at various times in this really neurotic, color-conscious country and world. I'm speaking now about the four

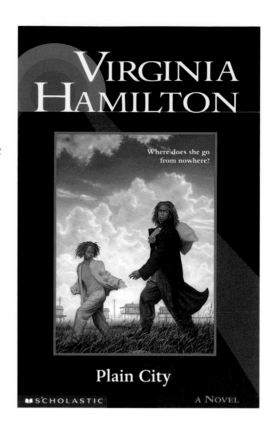

VIRGINIA HAMILTON

Where does she go from nowhere?

Plain City

SCHOLASTIC   A NOVEL

of us–my husband, and grown children and me. There are still places, in the White community as well as the Black, where I am not comfortable going with my husband. We do run into the gambit of hostilities at times. But usually, folks are pretty nice, quite easy with us. But we are able to talk about everything and come to clear conclusions about ourselves and our lives. We are all pretty well-adjusted. We take "no stuff from nobody!"

Your characters have striking names. How do you choose or create them?

Names of characters usually come to me out of character development. But often I get the names at the same time as or before the characters. I had the name M. C. Higgins for years in my head without knowing what it meant. Buhlaire came to me as soon as the character was born on the page. Zeely came out of thin air–I remember thinking hard for a name. I may have heard it, I don't know. But I think I created it. Brother Rush comes from a kid I met down south. His last name was Rush. I added the "Brother." And so forth, on and on. Names mean a lot in a book and should be chosen carefully.

You seem to employ the principle of Sankofa in much of your work. Your characters go back to "fetch" something important from the past that helps bring a resolution to a contemporary problem. Would you comment on that?

That's interesting, that "fetching" out of the past. I believe in the nexus, the connection to past lives and times. I can no more ignore my personal and historical heritage than I can ignore my own children. All Black people have an abundant and absolutely compelling historical past. I am a student of history. I believe in keeping it alive through story and through biography and the collections I do. I believe that through collecting material told by Black storytellers of long ago, I actually bring them to life,

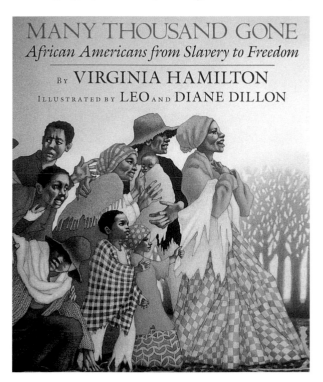

somewhat, while adding my voice–my experience and vision–to theirs. I truly believe that when I write of the past, as in the Anthony Burns book or *The People Could Fly* and *Many Thousand Gone*, I have touched the heart and hand of those long gone and brought them into our light of day.

You have written biographies, contemporary and historical fiction, and you have retold tales. Is a different mind set required for each genre?

Each genre plays well against the other. Collections are relief from the hard work of novel writing. Biographies and the historical reconstructions are the most difficult work I do. I adored doing the Burns book and *Paul Robeson*. The Du Bois biography nearly killed me. The man wrote every day of his life! And published everything, practically, that he wrote. Very difficult to put it all together. One has to actually feel as though one has become the person, when doing biography or reconstructions. One *is* that person. I was Anthony Burns as a child at the hiring ground.

I was in Boston awhile ago for the New England Booksellers Trade Show and I was actually in Faneuil Hall, revisiting that place that had been Anthony's jail. It gave me the shivers. All those portraits of great White men that line the great hall. Where is the portrait of Anthony Burns?

Do all your books require research?

Yes, all of them. Novels take less than most others. Sometimes, if I'm doing something difficult, I have to find out about a lot of different things. Everything has to be

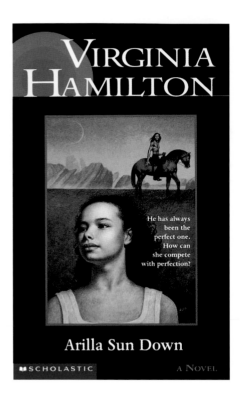

Arilla Sun Down

checked and rechecked. In *Arilla Sun Down*, I had to learn all about certain ponies, horses, their reactions; sleet storms, ice storms, Amerindian peoples. I actually studied the Cheyenne language. Other tribes as well. My Amerindian friends say I did a good job with James False Face and Shy Woman and Luze Montana. I certainly worked hard.

Many Black Americans don't know very much about their ancestors, or their family history beyond one or two generations. You seem to know quite a bit about your family heritage. Why?

Well then, it's a story, you see—one that I tell in a commentary in *The People Could Fly*. My grandfather Levi was a fugitive from slavery. His mother, Mary Cloud (Black and partly Patawatami Indian—thus, her last name, Cloud), brought him to a town near Yellow Springs (Jamestown) where he was raised by a friend. Obviously

Mary Cloud knew her way north. At any rate, she then disappeared. The story is that the owner brought her and her son north but made Mary return to slavery. No one knows for sure.

Years later, Levi moved to Yellow Springs as a young man, worked, bought a farm, and had 10 children. My mother was the oldest daughter. Every year, her father, Levi, sat his 10 children down, saying, "Listen, children, I want to tell you about slavery and how I ran from it. So then slavery will never happen to you."

Mother said this took place each year. Yet, she never quite told me exactly what he said. Very odd. But in a way, it has allowed me to create so many characters who have escaped chains of all kinds.

There are many family stories on my father's side as well. Dad's family was surnamed Auberchampsnoir. I'm not sure of the spelling. It was a New Orleans and Creole connection. Dad was a classical mandolinist, very accomplished. He had mandolin clubs that at the turn of the century played everywhere and were inte-grated—Black, White, male, and female. He was also a professional gambler, a wanderer across America and Canada. He and my mother spent their honeymoon in Nome, Alaska. Very weird characters! And great storytellers.

You have dedicated many of your books to individual members of your family. What role do family members play in the develop-ment of your work?

It's been a pleasure to be able to dedicate books to my relatives and friends. My children always like having a book in their names. I've dedicated books to my husband, editors, to my mother and father, also. *Cousins* was dedicated to my mother. Gram Tut in the nursing home in *Cousins* is only incidentally like my mother. She's pretty well a creation. But the nursing home experience is authentic. Mother spent the last three years of her life in the local Friends nursing home. I practically lived there during the day, so I got to know a lot of the folks and the routine. The book followed quite naturally. Mother lived to be 97 and *Cousins* is my ode to her.

You have used the term "Liberation Literature." What does that mean?

Through knowing the lives and struggles of others of our race in other times and trials, by reading about them, we experience their tribulations with them through words and language and feelings. We feel their bitter tears and re-live their progress toward individual freedom. Their forward progress is our own, too; and as they are liberated, by experiencing what they've gone through, we undergo a liberating catharsis. We have, therefore, a Liberation Literature through which we are bound together in time as one people.

What's the story behind your dedication in Her Stories: African American Folktales, Fairy Tales, and True Tales?

I dedicated it to "Our mothers and grandmothers . . . ," to all the women who took care of us and cared about what happened to "us," their children. They showed us the way is what I mean to say. They showed us

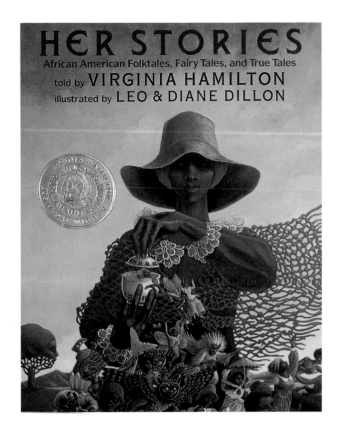

that caring was/is nurturing. All the women–the mothers, aunts, great-aunts, and grandmothers–were caring people, family people. They were proud, stubborn, and quite clannish and eccentric. They needed only one another for entertainment, story, conversation, love, and guidance. They protected us from the harsh world, until the time we, the children, were old enough to survive and prevail on our own. Many of us lit out for parts more interesting just as soon as we were old enough. But we always knew we had a home. We could always go home again. I left for 15 years while seeking my fortune in New York. When I found it (!) I came back home, where I live now, on land and across the road from land that has been in my family for generations. ■

Feel the Spirit

by Joyce Hansen
photograph by Austin Hansen

I was born in Charleston, South Carolina, in the year 1852.
The place of my birth and the conditions under which I was born
are matters over which, of course, I had no control . . . My great
grandfather came, or rather was brought, from Africa. It is said
he bore the distinguishing marks of royalty on his person and was
a fine looking man—fine looking for a Negro I believe is the
usual qualification . . . My father and my mother were both
under the "yoke," but were held by different families . . .

–from Samuel Williams's *Before the War and After the Union*

When I am writing historical pieces, the past often
becomes more real to me than the present, because
I must immerse myself in a particular period so that I
can write what I think I know. We will never know the
exact "truth"; knowing is not enough, anyway. At some point in
the writing you must find the connection that will help you feel
what a historical era was like. Facts and figures painstakingly
researched yield useful information, but this is just the bare
bones; you need flesh and blood to create life. For example, it is
estimated that Africa lost about 40 million people over the
course of five centuries of the slave trade. That is a devastating
number; however, when you read a detailed and painfully vivid
eyewitness account of the plundering of a village by slave raiders,
such a narrative has an impact that facts and figures cannot
generate. Multiply that one village by hundreds and thousands of
villages, and the horror assaults your consciousness.

Fortunately, I was raised by parents who used narratives to pass
on to their children their hard-won wisdom. My father, Austin,
used to tell us about his aunt in the Virgin Islands, who, while
everyone was trying to keep the house from sliding down a hill
during a hurricane, kept on baking her johnnycakes, flipping

them over the fire as the storm raged on and the house slid down the hill like a roller coaster. Moral: stick to what's important–never give up.

My mother, Lillian, frequently told of the time in 1920 when she and her sisters, Dorothy and Helen, and her brother, Harold (all very young children), had to sit quietly and respectfully in the parlor of their house in Charleston, South Carolina, and watch their grandfather as he lay on the cooling board, because, as was the custom, the deceased were placed on view in their homes, not in a funeral parlor. Moral: death is a part of life and we must not be afraid of death.

I suppose that since I grew up in a home full of stories (many embellished and just one sentence from a lie), I've always searched for the narrative in most things that I've read. As an adult writing historical fiction and nonfiction, I discovered the power of the slave narrative to help me internalize what American slavery might have been like.

And so I come to this picture of Samuel Williams–my mother's step-grandfather, a man born into slavery in 1852 in Charleston, South Carolina, a man whose gentlemanly ways, superior intelligence, and keen insight my mother often recalled. My mother also told me how he often recounted his experiences as a child held in slavery, and later as a freed young man who eventually ended up in Puritan New England, where he lived out his life. Sadly, however, when this old griot tried to tell his story, his voice mostly fell on the ears of a deaf tribe.

"Why do you want to go back so far?" the young people in his family would say to him.

"Daughter," he'd respond, "if you don't look back, you won't know how far you've traveled."

He knew the power of the narrative and the importance of the tale that he had to tell: his was a determined spirit and voice. So with my mother typing the manuscript for him, he self-published his narrative, under the pen name Sam Aleckson, in 1929 when he was about 79 years old: *Before the War and After the Union*.

I do not think many people read it, because his daughter, Susan Williams Cox, had a box full of copies of his book. Thank goodness she knew the treasure she possessed, otherwise I might never have gotten a copy. That was about 30 years ago, long before I started writing.

History became very real to me the first time I read Samuel Williams's slave narrative, written 64 years after the abolition of slavery. His voice and spirit broke through the sometimes stilted 19th-century prose, and I was captivated by his account of a world long gone, but still shaping us.

Though Samuel Williams and I are not related by blood, I must feel the same kind of strong kinship with him that my mother and father felt. My father took this photograph of him when Mr. Williams made one of his visits to New York City in the 1940s. Austin, with his own sense of history, fleshed out the old man's narrative with the camera's eye, knowing that this griot who had witnessed slavery ought to be venerated. Living history, he was. His voice should not have been stilled by those who wish to forget.

While it is sweet to forgive and forget, there are some things that should never be forgotten. If this humble narrative will serve to cause the youth of my people to take a glance backward, the object of the writer will have been attained. As Frederick Douglass has said, "How can we tell the distance we have come except we know the point from which we started?"

I reread Samuel Williams's narrative each time I write a historical piece–fiction or nonfiction–taking that pilgrimage back to his world and time, so that I can hear his voice, feel his spirit, and not forget. ■

I was born in Charleston, South Carolina, in the year 1852. The place of my birth and the conditions under which I was born are matters over which, of course, I had no control . . . My great grandfather came, or rather was brought, from Africa. It is said he bore the distinguishing marks of royalty on his person and was a fine looking man–fine looking for a Negro I believe is the usual qualification . . . My father and my mother were both under the "yoke," but were held by different families . . .

John Biggers
Baptism, 1989
Oil and acrylic on canvas
50 x 42 inches
Hampton University Museum
Hampton, VA

Long Distance Warriors, Dreamers & Rhymers

In memory of John Henry and Emma Jean Redmond

by Eugene B. Redmond
painting by John Biggers

O classical mammas & poppas: soular-centered lovers &
Parents of Drum, Scripture & Pyramid:
               Nile-cool & Benin-blue Songhaifiers:
      hip–& pre-Hip/Hop–diasporan daddies
          & *honey-in-the-rock divas:*
      ship-huddled & cattle-hurried
            across the Ethiopian Ocean. O epic parents:
Fine brown arks war-poised & prayerful. Long-distance Dreamers
& W.E.B.'s *souljahs* smelting ancestral ore
        into double-conscious Rhymes
        of epic Passage
            epic Pain
               epic Spillage:

Lo, you *stolen legacies* Rocking burdens beside the Mississippi
& creeping or racing
        like Ogun's archers & Harriet's scouts
           through *steal-away* nights:
Militantly upright, or shape-shifty, your *winged whisperings*
arming us with *clouds of joy* that "swing low" & "fetch high":
        Olmec & SoulTrek   Nat Turner & Sojourner
        Paul Laurence Dunbar & James Weldon Johnson
        Hughes' Blues   Mahalia & Maya   B.B. & CeCe
        Mary Bethune &   Henry Dumas &   Duke's Jive
        Zora Neale & Larry Neal   Cullen & Hayden
        Elijah & Umoja   Gwendolyn & Aretha
        Kenyatta & Mandela   Nyerere & Amiri   Nina & Sonia
        Toni & Terry   Malcolm & Jesse
        Katherine & Latifah   Juju & Jesus

        O parents of Mem/Wars & Love-Mergers: ritual (!) clickings
storefront-saviors   cornbread-fantasies   hambone & banjo
        railroad & gumbo   Thurgood's legions   King's cadres
of Orators ... O epic parents of mother-shore & father-ore
        smelting generations of fine brown arks
        into battle & prayer: *warriors dreamers rhymers.*

Ancient-Future Family

Knights of Endurance

by Leo and Diane Dillon

Ancient-Future Family Knights of Endurance

by Leo and Diane Dillon

This family portrait represents battles won and lost, and endurance through the ages.

In one hand the father holds a living staff, a symbol of support and protection, while he cradles in his other arm the infant, or new beginnings. The mother protects the book of knowledge, while their son raises the scales of justice.

They come from places we know or imagine.

They are the ancient-future.

They watch us.

About the Contributors

Tina Allen, a Los Angeles-based sculptor and writer, is the conceptual designer for the South African Statue of Liberty Project, for which she is organizing the erection of a 10-story statue of Nelson Mandela. She is also working on a 12-foot seated statue of Alex Haley in Knoxville, Tennessee, which will be the focal point of Haley Heritage Square.

John Biggers specializes in painting and sculpting African Americans and West Africans. *The Art of John Biggers: View fom the Upper Room* is a bountiful collection of reproductions of his paintings, sculptures, and drawings. His work can be viewed at the Hampton University Museum; the Wadsworth Atheneum in Hartford, Connecticut; The Museum of Fine Arts in Houston; and the North Carolina Museum of Art. He lives in Houston, Texas.

Tonya Bolden is the author of the novel *Just Family*, a spring 1996 Junior Library Guild selection; editor of the anthology *Rites of Passage: Stories About Growing Up by Black Writers from Around the World*, and co-author, with Vy Higginsen, of the novel *Mama, I Want to Sing*. Her first children's book is *Through Loona's Door: A Tammy and Owen Adventure with Carter G. Woodson*. She is a Harlemite who lives in the Bronx, New York.

Higgins Bond has illustrated eight children's books, among them: *When I Was Little* and *Susie King Taylor Destined to Be Free*, both published by Just Us Books, and *Toni Morrison: Author*. A graduate of Phillips University in Enid, Oklahoma, and Memphis College of Arts, Bond has also painted commemorative stamps of W. E. B. Du Bois and Jan Matzeliger for the United States Postal Service's Black Heritage Stamp Series. She lives in New Jersey.

Candy Dawson Boyd, professor of education at St. Mary's College of California at Moraga, has lectured nationwide on multiethnic education, reading/language arts, and children's literature. Her first book for young readers, *Circle of Gold* (1984), was chosen as a Coretta Scott King Honor Book. *Charlie Pippin*, *Forever Friends*, and *Daddy, Daddy, Be There* are among her other books for young people. Boyd lives in the San Francisco Bay area of California.

Gwendolyn Brooks became the first Black American to be awarded a Pulitzer Prize, which she won in 1950 for her second volume of poetry, *Annie Allen*. Among her many other honors, she was named Poet Laureate of Illinois in 1968, appointed Poetry Consultant to the Library of Congress 1985-1986, inducted into the Women's Hall of Fame in 1988, and given a Lifetime Achievement Award from the National Endowment for the Arts in 1989. In addition to some 20 books of poetry, Brooks is the author of several short stories, the novel *Maud Martha*, and the autobiographies *Report from Part One* and *Report from Part Two*. She lives in Chicago, Illinois.

Margery Wheeler Brown, a former educator, is the author of *AFRO-BETS® Book of Shapes*, *AFRO-BETS® Book of Colors*, and *Baby Jesus, Like My Brother*, an American Bookseller's 1995 "Pick of the List," all published by Just Us Books. Brown has also authored and/or illustrated *That Ruby*, *Yesterday I Climbed a Mountain*, and *The Second Stone*. She lives in East Orange, New Jersey.

Ashley Bryan is the author and/or illustrator of more than 30 books for children. His *Beat the Story Drum Pum Pum* was awarded a 1981 Coretta Scott King Award for Illustration. *I'm Going to Sing; Lion and the Ostrich Chicks and Other African Folk Tales;* and *All Night All Day: A Child's First Book of African-American Spirituals* are all Coretta Scott King Honor Books. He lives in Islesford, Maine.

Ron Ceasar, a self-taught photographer, owns and operates Ceasar Photography, a commercial photography business in his native Washington, D.C., where he lives with his wife and two children. His clients include Howard University and *Smithsonian*, *Emerge*, and *Black Enterprise* magazines.

Roland Charles is the founder and director of Black Photographers of California, Inc.; a founding board member of the Jazz Photographers Association; and director of the Black Gallery in Los Angeles. He is curator and one of the 10 photographers in the exhibition "Life in a Day of Black L. A.: The Way *We* See It," and co-editor of the show's companion book. Charles lives in southern California.

Floyd Cooper, who was born and raised in Tulsa, Oklahoma, has illustrated more than 15 children's books. *Grandpa's Face* was named an ALA Notable Book and a School Library Journal Best Book of the Year. *Brown Honey in Broomwheat Tea*, written by Joyce Carol Thomas, was a 1994 Coretta Scott King Honor Book for Illustration. Cooper also illustrated *Pass It On: African-American Poetry for Children* and *How Sweet the Sound: African-American Songs for Children*, both produced by Just Us Books, and *Jaguarundi* written by Virginia Hamilton. Among the books he has authored and illustrated is *Coming Home: From the Life of Langston Hughes*. He lives in New Jersey with his wife and sons, Noah and Dayton.

Pat Cummings received the 1984 Coretta Scott King Award for Illustration for *My Mama Needs Me*, written by Mildred Pitts Walter. Cummings has also illustrated *Chilly Stomach* and *Just Us Women*, and is the author and illustrator of *Jimmy Lee Did It* and *C.L.O.U.D.S.* This graduate of Pratt Institute in New York and member of the Graphic Artist's Guild lives with her husband in Brooklyn, New York.

Leo and Diane Dillon have illustrated more than two dozen books for young people. Their list of honors includes: two Caldecott Medals for *Why Mosquitos Buzz in People's Ears* and *Ashanti to Zulu*; three *New York Times* Best Illustrated Awards; four *Boston Globe-Horn Book* Awards; and the Society of Illustrators Gold Medal. *Her Stories: African American Folktales, Fairy Tales, and True Tales*, told by Virginia Hamilton, was a 1996 Coretta Scott King Honor Book for Illustration. The Dillons are the 1996 United States' nominees for the Hans Christian Andersen Medal. They live in New York City.

Tom Feelings has taught illustration in Ghana and was a professor of art at the University of South Carolina at Columbia, where he lives with his wife and daughter. Among the children's books Feelings has illustrated are: *To Be a Slave*, a 1969 Newbery Honor Book; *Moja Means One* and *Jambo Means Hello*, both Caldecott Honor Books; *Something on My Mind*, written by Nikki Grimes; *Soul Looks Back in Wonder*, winner of the 1994 Coretta Scott King Award for Illustration; and *The Middle Passage*, a *Publishers Weekly* Best Book of 1995, a *Booklist* Editors Choice for young adults, and winner of the 1996 Coretta Scott King Award for Illustration.

George Ford has illustrated more than two dozen books for young readers. Among them: *Muhammad Ali*; *Paul Robeson*; *Ray Charles*, for which he won the 1974 Coretta Scott King Award for Illustration; *AFRO-BETS® First Book About Africa*, *Bright Eyes, Brown Skin*, written by his wife, Bernette G. Ford and Cheryl Willis Hudson; *Jamal's Busy Day*, written by Wade Hudson; all published by Just Us Books. *The Hunter Who Was King*, adapted by Bernette G. Ford, and *The Story of Ruby Bridges* are among the more recent books Ford has illustrated. He lives in Brooklyn, New York, with his wife and daughter.

Roland Freeman, the founder and president of The Group for Cultural Documentation, has received Masters of Photography Visual Arts Fellowships from the National Endowment for the Arts and the Living Legend Award from the National Black Arts Festival. Freeman's books include *Something to Keep You Warm: Black American Quilts from the Mississippi Heartland*, *Stand by Me: African-American Expressive Culture in Philadelphia*, and *The Arabbers of Baltimore*. He lives in Washington, D.C.

Nikki Grimes is a poet, journalist, and author whose books for children and young adults include: *Growin'*; *Something on My Mind*, a 1979 Coretta Scott King Award winner and an ALA Notable Book; and *Meet Danitra Brown*. Her children's verse has appeared in *Cricket* magazine and in the anthologies *Bubbles: Poetry for Fun & Meaning*, *A World of Poetry*, and *Pass It On: African-American Poetry for Children*. Grimes's collection of poetry, *From a Child's Heart*, published by Just Us Books, features children's prayers to God. She lives in Seattle, Washington.

Virginia Hamilton is the author of some 40 books for young readers. Her 1974 novel, *M.C. Higgins, the Great*, was the recipient of a *Boston Globe-Horn Book* Award, a Lewis Carroll Shelf Award, a National Book Award, and a Newbery Medal. *The People Could Fly* and *Her Stories: African American Folktales, Fairy Tales, and True Tales*, both illustrated by Leo and Diane Dillon, received Coretta Scott King Awards. Hamilton has the distinction of being the first writer of books for young people to be awarded a MacArthur Fellowship. In 1992 she received the Hans Christian Andersen Medal U.S. for lifetime contributions to literature, and she was the recipient of the 1995 Laura Ingalls Wilder medal for her "substantial and lasting contribution to literature for children." She lives in Ohio with her husband, poet Arnold Adoff.

Austin Hansen, a prolific studio photographer and photojournalist, was born in 1910 and died in January 1996. From 1940 to 1987, he owned and operated a studio on West 135th Street in Harlem, where he produced a massive archive of photographs of life there. Before his death, he donated his full collection of 50,000 prints and negatives to Harlem's Schomburg Center for Research in Black Culture.

Joyce Hansen, who was born in the Bronx, New York, is the author of *Between Two Fires: Black Soldiers in the Civil War*. Her young adult novels include: *The Gift-Giver*; *Home Boy*; *Yellow Bird and Me*; *Out from This Place*; *Which Way to Freedom*, a 1987 Coretta Scott King Honor Book; and *The Captive*, a 1995 Coretta Scott King Honor Book and recipient of the 1995 Children's Book Award from the African Studies Association. In 1989 she received The Edgar Allan Poe Award from the Bronx County Historical Society. Hansen taught reading and language in the New York City pubic schools for 22 years and has been a part-time mentor at Empire State College. She lives in Columbia, South Carolina, with her husband.

Chester Higgins, Jr. has been a photographer for *The New York Times* since 1975. His work has also appeared in *Look*, *Time*, *Newsweek*, *Ebony*, and *Essence* magazines. Higgins's books include *Black Women*, *Drums of Life*, *Some Time Ago*, and *Feeling the Spirit: Searching the World for People of Africa*. Higgins makes his home in Brooklyn, New York.

Elizabeth Fitzgerald Howard, a former children's librarian at the Boston Public Library, is professor emeritus of library science at the University of West Virginia. She is the author of six children's books, including *Aunt Flossie's Hat (And Crab Cakes Later)*, illustrated by James E. Ransome, and *Chita's Christmas*, illustrated by Floyd Cooper. Her first, *The Train to Lulu's*, was an American Bookseller's "Pick of the List." *What's in Aunt Mary's Room* was a Junior Library Guild Selection for spring 1996. Howard lives in Pittsburgh, Pennsylvania, with her husband.

Toyomi Igus is the co-author of *Book of Black Heroes, Volume II: Great Women in the Struggle* and author of *When I Was Little, The Two Mrs. Gibsons,* and *Going Back Home: An Artist Returns to the South*. A veteran of west coast magazine publishing, Igus is co-editor of *Life in A Day of Black L.A.: The Way We See It*. She makes her home in Southern California with her husband and two children.

Angela Johnson is the author of more than a dozen books for children and young adults. Among them: *Tell Me a Story, Mama; When I Am Old with You; Joshua by the Sea; Joshua's Night Whispers;* and *The Aunt in Our House*. Her first book for young adults, *Toning the Sweep*, received the 1994 Coretta Scott King Award. A native of Tuskegee, Alabama, Johnson now makes her home in Kent, Ohio.

Bakari Kitwana is the political editor of *The Source: The Magazine of Hip Hop Music, Culture and Politics* and is the author of *The Rap on Gangsta Rap*. Kitwana writes music reviews for National Public Radio and lectures at colleges and universities across the country on rap music and Black youth culture. He lives in Wooster, Ohio.

E. B. Lewis, a graduate of Temple University's Tyler School of Art, began illustrating children's books in 1994. *Fire on the Mountain, The New King, Big Boy, Down the Road, The Magic Moonberry Jump Ropes,* and *Magid Fasts for Ramadan* are among his books. Lewis is a native of Philadelphia now living in Folsom, New Jersey.

Haki R. Madhubuti is the author/editor of more than 20 books of poetry and nonfiction, among them: *Black Men: Obsolete, Single, Dangerous?; Million Man March/Day of Absence: A Commemorative Anthology* (edited with Maulana Karenga); and *Groundwork: Selected Poems, 1966-1996*. Madhubuti is the founder of Third World Press and *Black Books Bulletin*, co-founder of the Institute of Positive Education/New Concept School in Chicago, and professor of English and director of the Gwendolyn Brooks Center at Chicago State University. In 1991 he received an American Book Award and was also named Author of the Year by the Illinois Association of Teachers of English. He lives in Chicago, Illinois, with his wife and children.

Patricia C. and Fredrick McKissack, Jr. are free-lance writers and editors who own McKissack & McKissack, a family business located in St. Louis, Missouri. Both graduates of Tennessee State University in Nashville, the McKissacks have collaborated on many books for children and young adults, among them: *A Long Hard Journey: The Story of the Pullman Porters*, winner of the 1990 Coretta Scott King Award; *Ain't I a Woman: The Story of Sojourner Truth*, winner of a *Boston Globe-Horn Book* Award; and *Black Diamond: The Story of the Negro Baseball Leagues*. The McKissacks have been married since 1964 and have three adult children.

Jeanne Moutoussamy-Ashe, a native of Chicago, is the author of *Daddy and Me*, a photographic essay about her late husband, U.S. tennis champion Arthur Ashe, and their daughter, Camera. *Daufuskie Island: A Photographic Essay* and *Viewfinders: Black Women Photographers* are her books for adults. Moutoussamy-Ashe's work has been exhibited in many one-woman shows in the United States and abroad and has appeared in various periodicals, including *People* and *Life* magazines and the *New York Times*. She lives in New York City.

Walter Dean Myers is the author of nearly 50 books for young readers. *Scorpions* was named a 1989 Newbery Honor Book and an ALA Notable Book. *Motown and Didi: A Love Story, Fallen Angels,* and *Now Is Your Time: The African-American Struggle for Freedom* all won Coretta Scott King Awards. Myers received the 1994 *School Library Journal*/ALSA Margaret A. Edwards Award for Outstanding Literature for Young Adults. He lives in Jersey City, New Jersey, with his wife.

John Pinderhughes has worked as a commercial photographer in New York City for two decades and has operated his own studio for more than 15 years. Recent clients include AT&T, Kodak, Pepsi-Cola, Chrysler, and General Foods. His fine art photography is represented in many major collections and has been on view at numerous shows, including the Museum of Modern Art's 1992 exhibition "Pleasures and Terrors of Domestic Comfort." Pinderhughes is the author of the cookbook *Family of the Spirit*. Born in Washington, D.C., and raised there and in Alabama and New Jersey, he now lives in New York City, with his wife and children.

Brian Pinkney has illustrated many books for children. They include: *The Ballad of Belle Dorcas*, a 1990 Parents' Choice selection; *Where Does the Trail Lead*, winner of a 1991 Golden Kite Honor Award; *Sukey and the Mermaid*, an ALA Notable Book and a Coretta Scott King Honor Book for 1993; *Alvin Ailey* and *Seven Candles for Kwanzaa*, both written by his wife Andrea Davis Pinkney; and *Faithful Friend*, a 1996 Caldecott Honor Book. He and his wife and child live in Brooklyn, New York.

Myles Pinkney is a free-lance photographer who graduated from Marist College with a degree in communication. He now owns and operates Timeless Images, a photography business, in Poughkeepsie, New York. His work has been featured in various shows and exhibits. He is presently working on several book projects, including *It's Raining Laughter* by Nikki Grimes and *Can You Imagine?* by Patricia C. McKissack.

James E. Ransome has illustrated more than a dozen books, among them: *Do Like Kyla* and *The Girl Who Wore Snakes*, both written by Angela Johnson; *Aunt Flossie's Hat (And Crab Cakes Later)*, by Elizabeth Fitzgerald Howard; *Uncle Jed's Barbershop*; and *Ziggy and the Black Dinosaurs*, published by Just Us Books. *The Creation*, his illustrated interpretation of James Weldon Johnson's poem, received the 1995 Coretta Scott King Award for Illustration. He lives in upstate New York with his wife and children.

Eugene B. Redmond, former contributing editor to the *East St. Louis Monitor* newspaper and *Confrontation: A Journal of Third World Literature*, is a poet, playwright, and educator. He was named Poet Laureate of East St. Louis in 1976, the year his book *Drumvoices: The Mission of Afro-American Poetry* was published. His books of poetry include *Rivers of Bones and Flesh and Blood* and *The Eye in the Ceiling*. Among his honors are two American Book Awards. Redmond lives in Missouri.

Anna Rich received her B.F.A. from Rhode Island School of Design and has served as the New York chapter chairperson of the Graphic Artists Guild. Among the books she has illustrated are: *Joshua's Masai Mask, Saturday at the New You, Little Louis and the Jazz Band*, and *Annie's Gifts*, published by Just Us Books. A native of the Bronx, New York, Rich now lives in Elmont, New York, with her husband.

Faith Ringgold is well known for her painted story-quilts, soft sculptures, and masks. Her books for children include *Tar Beach*, winner of the 1992 Coretta Scott King Award for Illustration and a Caldecott Honor Award; *Aunt Harriet's Underground Railroad*; *Dinner at Aunt Connie's House*; and *My Dream of Martin Luther King*. A native of Harlem, Ringgold now divides her time between homes in La Jolla, California, and Englewood, New Jersey.

David J.A. Sims is head illustrator and co-owner of Big City Comics, Inc., publisher of the nationally distributed comic book series *Brotherman: Dictator of Discipline*. His book credits include: *Sniffy Blue: Ace Crime Detective* by Walter Dean Myers. A native of Philadelphia, Pennsylvania, Sims now lives in North Bergen, New Jersey, with is wife and two children.

Bweela Steptoe, daughter of the highly acclaimed children's book author/illustrator John Steptoe, is completing her bachelor's degree in fashion design at Fashion Institute of Technology in New York City and works part-time as an assistant fashion designer. She makes her home in Brooklyn, New York.

Javaka Steptoe, son of author/illustrator John Steptoe, is a graduate of Cooper Union in New York City. He is a free-lance artist who does graphic design, editorial illustration, and creative art for video productions. He is presently illustrating a collection of poetry about fathers. Steptoe lives in Brooklyn, New York.

Eleanora E. Tate, a native of Canton, Missouri, is the author of *A Blessing in Disguise*, an American Bookseller's "Pick of the List"; *Thank You, Dr. Martin Luther King, Jr.!*, a Child Study Association "Children's Book of the Year"; and several other books for young readers. Her first published book, *Just An Overnight Guest* is scheduled for re-release by Just Us Books in spring 1997. Tate lives in Morehead City, North Carolina.

Joyce Carol Thomas was born in Ponca City, Oklahoma, the state where much of her fiction and poetry is set. She was honored with a National Book Award for her first novel, *Marked by Fire*. Thomas received the Poet Laureate for Life Award from the Oklahoma Center for Poets and Writers following the publication of her Coretta Scott King Honor Book, *Brown Honey and Broomwheat Tea*, illustrated by Floyd Cooper. Her book, *Gingerbread Days*, is a collection of poetry. She lives in Berkeley, California.

Glennette Tilley Turner, an historian and educator with a master's degree in children's literature, was an elementary school teacher for nearly 25 years. She is the author of a biography, *Lewis Howard Latimer*; *Take a Walk in Their Shoes*, a collective biography with skits; and *Running for Our Lives*, about the Underground Railroad. She lives in Wheaton, Illinois, with her husband.

Mildred Pitts Walter is the author of more than a dozen books for children and young adults, among them: *My Mama Needs Me* and *Two Too Much*, both illustrated by Pat Cummings; *Brother to the Wind*, illustrated by Leo and Diane Dillon; *Justin and the Best Biscuits in the World*, winner of the 1987 Coretta Scott King Award; *Darkness*; *Second Daughter, The Story of a Slave Girl*; and *Mississippi Challenge*. Walter lives in Denver, Colorado.

Richard Wesley has penned numerous works for the stage and screen. His plays include *The Black Terror*, *The Sirens*, *The Mighty Gents*, and *The Talented Tenth*. Among his screenplays are *Uptown Saturday Night*, an NAACP Image Award winner; *Let's Do It Again*; *Fast Forward*; and *Native Son*. He makes his home in Montclair, New Jersey, where he and his wife raised two children.

■ ■ ■

Wade Hudson and Cheryl Willis Hudson founded the publishing company Just Us Books in 1988. Cheryl Willis Hudson is a graphic designer and author whose books include *AFRO-BETS® ABC Book*; *AFRO-BETS® 123 Book*; *Bright Eyes, Brown Skin* (with Bernette G. Ford); *Good Morning, Baby*; *Good Night, Baby*; and *Hold Christmas in Your Heart*. Among the many books Wade Hudson has written are: *AFRO-BETS® Book of Black Heroes from A to Z* (with Valerie Wilson Wesley); *Five Brave Explorers*; *I Love My Family*; *Jamal's Busy Day*; and *Pass It On: African-American Poetry for Children*, a 1993 American Bookseller's "Pick of the List." The Hudsons are the editors of *How Sweet the Sound: African-American Songs for Children* and *Kids' Book of Wisdom: Quotes from the African-American Tradition*. They live in East Orange, New Jersey, with their children.

Acknowledgments

The editors wish to thank the following people and sources for permission to use material in this collection:

page 10 (top) Family photographs, courtesy of Margery Wheeler Brown; (bottom) "Sunlight and Zinnias," dry brush watercolor, copyright © Margery Wheeler Brown, courtesy of the artist.

page 12 John L. Wheeler retired in 1950 as vice president and agency director of the Atlanta office of the North Carolina Mutual Insurance Company. By his side is his wife, Margaret Hervey Wheeler. Photo courtesy of Margery Wheeler Brown.

page 13 The Wheeler family home on Johnson Avenue, Atlanta, Georgia, was sold to Ebenezer Baptist Church in the early 1960s and became the residence of then associate pastor Rev. Martin Luther King, Jr. and his family. Photo courtesy of Margery Wheeler Brown.

page 18 (top) US County designs by Bweela and Javaka Steptoe; (bottom left) portrait of Javaka Steptoe; (bottom right) portrait of Bweela, used as a model for cover of John Steptoe's *Mufaro's Beautiful Daughters*. All photos courtesy of Bweela and Javaka Steptoe.

pages 20, 21, 23 Photos courtesy of Bweela and Javaka Steptoe.

page 24 "My Neighborhood," drawing, copyright © Javaka Steptoe, courtesy of the artist.

page 25 "Tiger Shoes," designed by Bweela Steptoe, courtesy of the artist.

page 44 Photo courtesy of Gwendolyn Brooks.

pages 44-45 "Home" is exerpted from *Report from Part One* by Gwendolyn Brooks. Copyright © 1973 by Gwendolyn Brooks (Broadside Press). Used by permission of the author.

page 49 and 51 Illustrations from *The Dark Thirty: Southern Tales of the Supernatural* and *Alvin Ailey* by Brian Pinkney, copyright © by Brian Pinkney, courtesy of the artist.

page 59 "Proud Father and Son," by Tina Allen, courtesy of the artist. Photo by Philip Ghee.

page 61 Photo of Mr. and Mrs. Sam Dance, courtesy of Bakari Kitwana.

pages 63-69 "A Personal Journey: Race, Rage, and Intellectual Development" from *Claiming Earth: Race, Rage, Rape, Redemption: Blacks Seeking a Culture of Enlightened Empowerment* by Haki R. Madhubuti. Copyright © 1994 by Haki R. Madhubuti (Third World Press). Used by permission of the author.

page 71 Photo of Jurdine Adkins as a teenager, courtesy of Wade Hudson.

page 76 "Smiley and Sylvia Fletcher's Family at Daily Prayer, Philadelphia, PA, 1988," copyright © by Roland Freeman, courtesy of the photographer.

pages 80-81 Family photos, courtesy of Lillian Watson Willis and Cheryl Willis Hudson.

page 83 Letters and photo, courtesy of Cheryl Willis Hudson.

page 84 (top) Photo of the Shores family, Nebraska State Historical Society. Used by permission. (bottom left) Photo of Lydia and Walter Holm(e)s, courtesy of Glennette Tilley Turner; (bottom right) facsimile of patent from U.S. Patent Office.

page 92 "The Bitter Nest Part 2: The Harlem Renaissance Party, 1988" by Faith Ringgold, courtesy of the artist.

page 108 Portrait of Virginia Hamilton, copyright © by Ron Rovtar.

pages 114 and 117 Portrait of Samuel Williams, copyright © by Austin Hansen. Schomburg Center for Research in Black Culture, Austin Hansen Collection. Used by permission of the photographer.

page 118 "Baptism," by John Biggers, 1989. Hampton University Museum, Hampton, VA. Used by permission.

Contributors' photo credits:
Tina Allen photo © by Spees Powell
John Biggers photo copyright © by Earlie Hudnall, Jr.
Ashley Bryan photo by Susan Valdina.
Roland Charles photo copyright © by Mike Jones, Los Angeles, CA.
Leo and Diane Dillon photo by Pat Cummings.
Tom Feelings photo by Dianne Johnson-Feelings.
Roland Freeman, self-portrait, 1992, copyright © 1992.
Nikki Grimes photo copyright © 1993 by Joelle Petit Adkins.
Austin Hansen photo by Jaribu Bobo, copyright © 1991, courtesy of the African Diaspora Youth Development
    Foundation, St. Thomas, V.I.
Joyce Hansen photo copyright © by Austin Hansen.
Chester Higgins photo © 1994 by Betsy Kissam.
Toyomi Igus photo copyright © by Roland Charles.
Brian Pinkney photo copyright © by Myles Pinkney.
Faith Ringgold photo by Grace Welty.
Eleanora E. Tate photo copyright © by Zack Hamlett, III.
Richard Wesley photo courtesy of Graham Brown.

Executive Editors: Wade Hudson and Cheryl Willis Hudson
Design Director: Cheryl Willis Hudson
Project Editor: Tonya Bolden
Editorial Support: Toyomi Igus
Copyeditor: Chérie Francis
Book Design: Carol T. Jenkins/Jenkins Graphics

The text was set in Galliard roman.
The display types were set in Architecture and Charme.

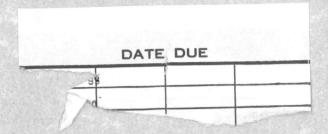